my cool® houseboat.

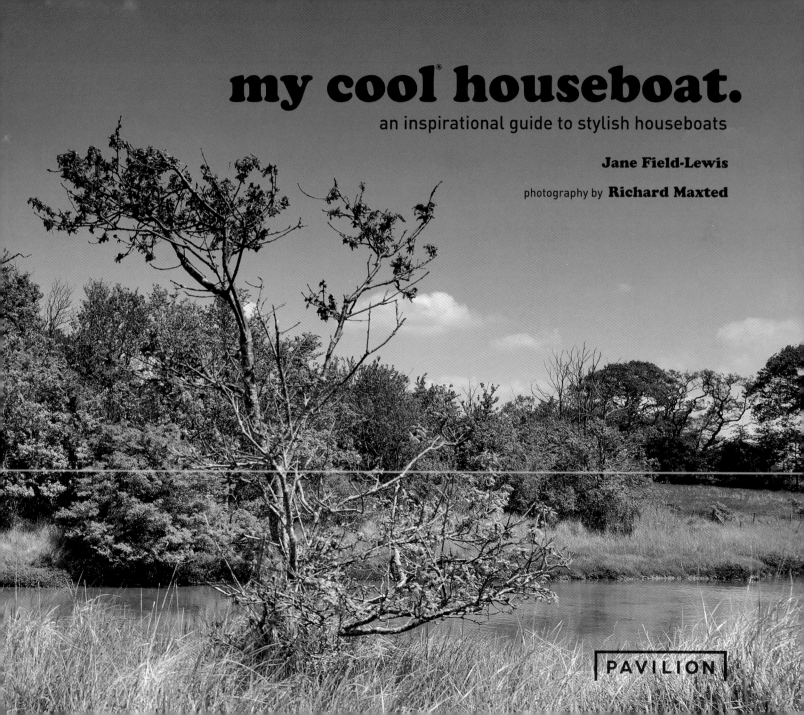

my cool houseboat.

an inspirational guide to stylish houseboats

Jane Field-Lewis

photography by **Richard Maxted**

PAVILION

contents

introduction

There's an innate romanticism and appeal about boats and messing about on the water – the sense of freedom, of escape and of being part of something much bigger and more elemental. A surprising number of people are now electing to live on boats and transform them into stylish and comfortable homes or even thriving businesses.

When I started climbing aboard the cool houseboats featured in this book, I felt slightly nervous. Although I was aware of the drift towards living on the water, I am a land dweller, unfamiliar with water, and I didn't feel confident on boats – I was out of my usual comfort zone. However, I was soon sucked into this new watery world and started to feel more at home in this unique experience. I was lucky enough to stay on some of the boats and felt entranced by the hypnotic view of the lapping water close up through the porthole windows, the gorgeous light and the gentle rocking of the boat at night. Life aboard is magical, comforting and reassuring – it takes us back to the basics.

For a long while the canal networks in many large cities, such as London, Amsterdam and Berlin, have been popular with boating aficionados, but they were often located, by default, in hard-living old industrial areas. They had their own distinctive aesthetic but were often neglected, their run-down towpaths separated from passing foot traffic. However, something interesting happened in London – the building of the facilities for the 2012 Olympic Games meant that many canal boat homes were temporarily moved away from development sites and into smarter inner-city areas. With the increase in the number of boats and people, the canals became safer and inspired more folk to consider embracing a new life on the water. Now, it's a blossoming community, with an exciting renewed energy, and there are funky shops, hip bars and cool homes that are all based on narrow boats.

I've seen similar scenarios in my travels across Europe with photographer Richard Maxted. We noticed a new trend in our conversations: 'this would be great for weekends' started creeping into our dialogue, and even 'if I had a boat I'd have this one'. In Copenhagen, we saw how the old shipyards are now thriving communities of boat homes, a short cycle ride away from the city centre. In Amsterdam, the ultimate water city, boat life has spread beyond the central canals to other waterways, and their long shipbuilding history is alive and well, creating new homes on the water. Conventional city living is expensive and we all need a home – preferably one that will give us joy and be as beautiful as possible. For many people, creating a home within a boat is the new affordable way to achieve just that.

In the course of researching, writing and photographing this book, I loved discovering and exploring the individual expressions of style, whether of small creative projects or larger more ambitious ones. By taking a considered look at them photographically and narrating the story of their realisation, both in human effort and in a design context, I can not only share them with you but also, hopefully, delight and inspire you.

Undoubtedly, austerity was the key to a new appreciation of the authentic, the genuine and the affordable style that is a feature of all my books, but the benefits experienced by the boat owners – like those of the sheds, caravans, campervans and kitchens featured in earlier titles in this series – are not going to disappear. Rather, they will grow into an even more confident expression of style. People are feeling freer and seeking opportunities for alternative less expensive ways to start businesses, to use their available space more creatively, to restore and re-develop the forgotten, the previously unfashionable and neglected and to have some fun and enjoy this new-found creative freedom.

In this same spirit, we looked far afield to source some amazing houseboats and take a peek at what their intrepid owners had achieved: within the UK, Denmark, Finland, Germany, France, the Czech Republic, Australia and the United States. From converted ferryboats to weekend retreats and disused freight barges, as well as redundant oil rig escape pods that are now hotel rooms and the most desirable and innovative of the architect-designed new builds. Within all these spaces, style and design haven't been forgotten and they live on in an expressive and inspirational way.

I hope you are inspired by the beautiful images of the boats, and that your spirits will be lifted by the motivational and incredible stories of their highly creative owners. This book has been an enormous pleasure and a privilege to produce. I'm grateful for the opportunity and I hope you enjoy it, too.

architectural

The boats featured in the following pages wear their strong architectural concepts, their shapes, their function, their design and inspiration proudly. Many houseboats are the result of conversions of other vessels, or are modular floating homes, but these vessels are innovative and different. New builds, purpose-designed, often in unconventional forms, in incongruous locations, they all represent a very modern and fresh approach to living on the water.

Makoko floating school is a visionary piece of floating architecture sited in the Lagos lagoon in West Africa. Its Amsterdam-based architect has created a community structure that can accommodate climatic water level changes and which is accessed only by canoe. It stands tall and airy, adjacent to the poor community it serves, with a non-threatening and benevolent presence.

Exactly the opposite in scale, the diminutive Finnish-designed, angular Camley Street shelters on the canal network in inner-city London, serve equally their local community of office workers and schoolchildren. Instead of feeling isolated in their air-conditioned glass, brick and concrete buildings, they can wander down to the canal and enjoy the peace and tranquillity of this beautiful shelter, feeling close to nature in an urban landscape.

And, of course, there's the jaw-dropping Exbury Egg, floating in its tidal estuary in an area of exceptional natural beauty. Although it is quite surreal, like a prop in a 1960s sci-fi film or a Terry Gilliam movie, this giant wooden egg looks strangely at home. I absolutely love it – it's so substantial and real. A triumph in many respects: its concept, design, realisation and state-of-the-art architecture have been melded with age-old boat-building techniques.

Inspiration is key here – looking at the required function, not being frightened to turn one's back on convention, and finding sustainable materials and methods to create these wonders. Creatively invigorating, they lift our spirits.

viewpoint shelters

This is more of a floating structure than a true boat, but it's still an interesting interpretation of how to integrate the waterside into everyday life. *Viewpoint* is a set of three different-shaped, triangular, open-sided shelters, sited on the edge of the Regents Canal in the Kings Cross area of London.

The simple multi-purpose floating structures were designed to provide an outdoor classroom, a habitat for birds and bats and a quiet comptemplative spot where the local office workers could take a break. Using materials that echo the construction of the local canal boats, the outer surface of the triangular pods are covered in rusty steel whereas their interiors are clad horizontally in wood with integral wooden seating benches.

Designed for the London Wildlife Trust by the Finnish architects Erkko Aart, Arto Ollila and Mikki Ristola (AOR), the idea for the shape came from 'the rocky islets and islands of the Nordic Sea' – places of sanctuary for escaping the treadmill of everyday life. They hoped that these structures would give Londoners a similar experience. Their other inspiration was the traditional Finnish triangular Laavus shelters, built of tree branches, moss, pelts or leaves, that face away from prevailing winds and are used on fishing and hunting trips.

style notes

This unique floating structure is multi-functional and can be perceived as an observation platform, a place for conversation or for contemplation and respite from city life, or even as a moored boat. Ingeniously designed, the separate but relating pods are like a piece of origami that has unfolded to enable people to enter. The walls have triangular peepholes for adults and children to watch the wildlife. The floor surface between the pods is made of concrete imprinted with created animal tracks.

The shelters sensitively harness the urban environment around them, reflecting the fragmented buildings and angles of the cityscape. They are incredibly inspirational, challenging our perceptions about the possibilities of floating structures and how they can become part of everyday life on the water.

What the pods offer us is the opportunity to spend time on or near the water, and to share the restful experience of boat dwellers – the quiet breeze, the sound of the water flowing through the locks, the swans, kingfishers and wildlife on the canal and, most importantly, a sense of tranquillity and temporary escape from the stresses of modern city life.

exbury egg

This extraordinary floating structure was custom-built as a temporary home and working studio for the artist Stephen Turner. For one year only, he is using this self-sustaining workspace and shelter, with its integral storage and display areas, as a base for artistic exploration, striving to achieve a more empathetic relationship with nature.

The tethered 'egg' rises and falls with the tides, and weathers the vagaries of the passing seasons in a tidal creek in the estuary of the Beaulieu River. It's a triumph in terms of appraising the way in which we live and how we consider sustainability. It was conceived for a design competition to create a structure that would welcome and display the effects of weathering, above and below the waterline. Wendy Perring, the egg's architect, says: 'The egg is a statement, a thing of beauty, but it is also by its very nature and in its construction really low-energy. It was built, as much as possible, from recycled material and it doesn't need much energy to maintain or run it. That was our intention from the beginning.'

This project was facilitated by a team of skilled professionals, including Spud (the project managers), a naval architect and a boat builder. It effortlessly combines engineering, art, design and architecture in an innovative way. Constructing this complex 3-D shape out of 2-D materials presented creative and practical challenges for the team. Making the two halves of the egg was similar to building the hull of a yacht. They were constructed in layers, leaving the outer cedar wood layer unfinished to accept the forces of nature. Inside is a waterproof layer of glass epoxy and below that an inner cedar layer. The two halves were joined together, and a circular window was inserted in the upper part with two access doors. Stephen has created another small round observation hole for watching wildlife.

style notes

Fitted out modestly, the egg is a functional and practical living space, measuring just 6 x 3m (20 x 10ft) but offering enough suitable workspace for Stephen to carry out his tasks plus sufficient living space to reasonably fend for himself. It accommodates a bed, a stove, a desk and a wet room. Any power for charging camera batteries or a laptop is provided by solar energy.

Visually, this simple elemental form is stunningly appropriate yet unexpected. The shift in context and proportion, and the man-made element of its creation, is deeply rooted in nature. It is, in every way, a wake-up call for us all. Things can look different and be different, and we don't always have to follow conventional form in design or in our behaviour. It is a privilege to have the experience of the egg, to cast your tired eyes on it and to feel invigorated. It is a thing of great cleverness and beauty.

This floating school building was developed in the stilt-based fishing village of Makoko in the Lagos lagoon in Nigeria. Facing the challenges of climate change and living not on dry land but in tidal waters, this poor community has neither roads nor infrastructure. The residents live in shanty-type buildings built on wooden piles driven into the estuary bed. The village has expanded rapidly and it needed a new school for the growing number of children. Building a conventional land-based building was impossible, and this innovative structure was designed by the Amsterdam-based architectural studio NLÉ, founded by Nigerian-born architect Kunle Adeyemi.

makoko floating school

The building serves several functions and can be used as an event space, market or clinic as well as a school. With the help of non-governmental organisations (NGOs), it was built by a team of local builders and residents using eco-friendly bamboo and off-cuts of wood from a nearby saw mill. Stability and balance are achieved by the triangular structure, with its low centre of gravity. Access is only by canoe. The lower level is a play space for the children, but out of school hours it becomes a community space for the local residents; the middle floor can be divided variously into two to four classrooms accommodating between 60 and 100 pupils; and on the upper floor is a small, semi-enclosed group workshop.

Construction began with the base, buoyancy being achieved by using locally sourced and readily available empty blue plastic barrels. The economical A-frame-shaped building stands 10m (32ft) high to the ridge. Its open slatted side walls provide natural ventilation, while electricity-generating photovoltaic panels are fitted to the roof area. It has inclusive technologies for waste reduction, a rainwater catchment system and sewage treatment.

style notes

Described by the architect as 'planting a seed' – one that grows, recycles waste and harvests water – this extraordinary building has an acute sense of its location, responding to the specific needs of the local community as well as the environment and changes in the water level. Stylish but relatively low tech, it addresses both issues in a practical and aesthetic way. Rather than convert an existing hull or vessel and add a super-structure, this is a minimalist but coherent structure that starts from scratch on a simple raft-type base.

Adeyemi believes that 'water is an important part of a recipe for a beautiful city', and all countries, no matter whether they are first or third world, need to recognise the importance of managing climate change. This process can start at grass roots level by communities looking within themselves to find effective solutions. On his first visit to Makoko he was amazed at how the local residents had built so much out of so little. With no roads and no land, he saw this as a model for how African coastal villages might develop. In Makoko the only infrastructure

is the water, and as he looked at the simple, basic homes of the settlement he realised that although they fulfilled their purpose they faced huge challenges.

Adeyami wanted to help, to learn and give something back to the community. He started by looking at the local school that regularly flooded. Speaking to the local experts who had built the houses on stilts, and pooling expertise from the Netherlands and their advanced technology of water dwelling, he realised that he could create a new school on a flotation device. It was a hybrid solution of local and global technology, about learning how to live with water, and how to create a new sustainable model for a coastal African water city.

Looking at the building as an integral part of its environment, it is majestic, a colossal piece of architecture. Like a piece of beautifully intricate sculpture, its open slatted wooden sides, tall apex and low centre of gravity all add a powerful presence to the landscape. It is Parthenaic – a forum for everyone and the living heart of the community.

san francisco floating house

The Golden Gate Bridge is one of the most famous sights in the world – a glowing red super-structure spanning the 1.6-km (1-mile) wide channel that separates the San Francisco Peninsula from Marin County. Not content with simply ogling it from their houseboat, Sarah and Kimo Bertram wanted it to inform their home's ambitious design. Their front door and the striking circular staircase ascending to the kitchen-dining-living area are painted the exact same colour. It's a quirk that helps anchor this boat firmly to its locality. More than that, such attention to detail is a hallmark of the entire residence.

Frustrated after failing to secure a more conventional home, the couple defected to the water after spotting an ad for a furnished houseboat to rent. They paid a visit, fell in love and ended up buying it. But, says Kimo, the dream was always to create something new. And so began their journey from a 1970s-style vacation home, complete with fish painted on the wall, to a bespoke abode – a project spanning some eight months and a few crossed fingers, too, when the land-built, loft-style erection was floated for the first time. Fortunately, it stayed upright and Sarah and Kimo could start unpacking boxes during the tow across the bay to their permanent mooring. The completion couldn't have come at a better time as the couple were expecting their first child. Meanwhile, their former houseboat was donated to a local charity focused on creating affordable residential solutions in the city.

Their floating home is moored in a charming backwater canal with an industrial heritage that helped inspire the boat's defining saw-toothed roof and tall casement windows. They flood the interior with light and give generous views across the water to the city beyond. It's the coolest place to live in San Francisco, Kimo assures his visitors. 'You feel like you're in the middle of paradise and you've got life that you don't see normally'.

style notes

Sarah and Kimo's architect, Robert Nebolon, performed a small miracle in maximising every inch of available space within their three-level 195 sq m (2,100 sq ft) home. Captain's beds allow drawer space underneath; the dining room table has a built-in window seat with storage; and the desk and computer centre doubles as a buffet table. Nothing about this boat feels cramped. A neutral palette and love affair with natural light accentuate the proportions. The staircase is open, maximising light and air between the floors, down to the below-waterline basement.

Upstairs is open-plan but each saw-tooth roof form expresses the function of the space below. One is placed directly over the dining room/kitchen area, while the other is above the living area. The distinctive roof profile is one of Robert's favourite features. It not only looks smart but it's a canny design, too, with the option of installing solar panels and acting as a rainwater drainage solution. And it informs the unusual window formations. Mixing small panes with over-sized panels, they extend all the way to the ceiling so the light washes evenly across it.

Neither Sarah nor Kimo are strangers to water – it's in their genes. Kimo has a passion for surfing, while his wife is the daughter of an amateur boat builder. The couple make waterways living look easy. Sometimes you just have to go with the flow, according to Sarah, and it's sound advice for other families looking to make the jump from terra firma to riverbank. Rather than over-thinking the move, Sarah and Kimo just did it. And in the process they've pulled something quite magical out of a box-like concrete barge. They've built a dream home.

eclectic

Living on the water rather than the land and in an idiosyncratic space inevitably leads to freedom of expression in lifestyle and design. None of the rooms in the boats featured in the following pages are regularly shaped – indeed, several of them have no straight walls at all. The way in which the spaces are lit is also unusual: a creative approach is called for when light has to be reflected off the water surface, usually through small porthole windows and open hatches. The limited, open-plan interiors dictate the overall look, which needs to work throughout all the spaces of each boat. All of this, coupled with the character of the owners, allows their individuality and freedom to shine through.

A canal narrowboat in the shadow of the Olympic Park has been refurbished to become the London home of Clio and Bryn, fitted out with up-cycled furniture from their thriving business. Although the *African Queen* in Berlin is no longer Imke's permanent home, its clean light, wooden floors and survivalist nature – amazingly, it has sunk twice – give it a truly unique character. A watchful statue of the Buddha sits on a windowsill, gazing into the boat, which is now used as the base for her yoga and therapy sessions.

And in Copenhagen Jesper and Jette's boat has been refurbished with reclaimed building materials. The kitchen is a funky mix of colourful old units sourced from the time of the old Eastern Bloc, and the walls are a vertical patchwork of different painted pieces of wood cut from old doors that were not good enough to use on their own – and the ladder to access the upper level is made from two ladders from builders' scaffolding welded together.

This refreshing and inspiring collection of houseboats is more than just a selection of vessels that reflect the eclectic tendencies and creative talents of their owners. The boats featured are also purposeful and functional, exuding their own very special and unique style.

clio the muse

Clio and her husband Byrn started their home-owning career with a two-bedroom flat in an upwardly mobile part of London. But when they wanted to upgrade, it was a huge jump to a larger flat in a better location and gaining an extra bedroom would cost at least double.

Clio's solution was to turn things on their head. She had always wanted to live in France, so the couple bought an eight-bedroom *manoir*, which doubles as a holiday home and off-season rental business while they're staying on *Jessie*, their one-bedroom narrow boat in London. Moored in a basin in a very hip and up-and-coming area not far from the City and the Olympic Park, it makes a great crash pad when they're in the UK.

When they acquired the boat, it was in good condition, but they still commissioned an out-of-the-water survey. They wanted to be sure they weren't buying a wreck as well as plan for future work. Constant maintenance is essential and rust can be kept in check only by regular re-painting and using epoxy black on the hull.

Jessie is a one-bedroom, 22-year-old, 19m (62ft) long and 2m (6ft 10in) wide narrowboat. Its mooring supplies everything you need: mains water and electricity, a laundry, wood store, bike shed and barbecue area – the boat even has wi-fi. The main living and kitchen space is open-plan and full of light with hatches on both sides. More importantly, it feels good – somewhere the couple can feel at home. Clio works as an up-cycler of furniture, and offers an interior design service, using her pieces. Her enviable lifestyle didn't just land in her lap – she formerly worked as a headhunter, up-cycling furniture as a hobby. Eventually, the day came when she thought honestly about her future and asked herself: 'Can I see myself doing this for the next 10 years?' The answer was a clear 'no'. Taking voluntary redundancy gave her the opportunity to carve out a new lifestyle and career.

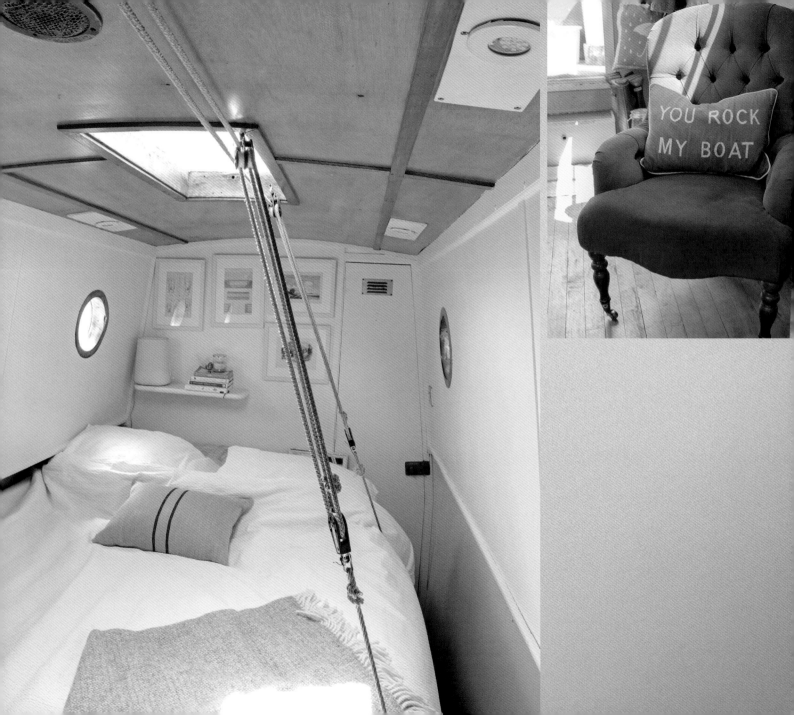

style notes

The simple layout had a big appeal for Clio. She was looking for an extra-long boat with one open-plan living space and a separate bedroom and bathroom – it's the size of a modest one-bedroom flat. The sitting area is calm and tranquil with Cole & Sons wallpaper extended through the length of the entire room above the gunnel rail and a cool grey paint below it. The floor was sanded back to the natural wood tone and sealed.

The sofa was built from pallets and plywood off-cuts – a padded, decorated storage chest, big enough to store Bryn's skis. The cushions were covered with fabric courtesy of Bryn's mum, and Clio recycled some vintage tea towels from a car-boot sale in France into throw cushions. The slate grey armchair is another up-cycled piece. Purchased for a song, it was an awful 1980s pink, but Clio transformed it into a lovely slate grey with fabric spray.

The storage solution was another of Clio's creations, using old crates with some of the back slats removed to allow for wires. A four-section cubby hole storage unit was made by fixing two fruit crates together. In the bedroom, a system of rope pulleys supports half the bed and lifts/folds it up and down. The non-moving part is built on storage drawers.

The bathroom has a half bath and shower, seawater toilet and small round sink. All Clio had to do was change the colours and add shelves for additional storage. The kitchen has a good area of workspace and mains water (the water tank on the boat needs weekly filling from the supply from the mooring pontoon). The cooker runs off bottled gas.

Living on a boat in the city has many benefits. When you fancy a weekend away, you can just set off from your city mooring, taking your house with you, and travel up the London river and canal system, stopping at hip bars and cafés on your way out of town.

The moment when Jesper decided to buy this boat was instinctive and instantaneous. It was owned by friends, who had purchased it as a renovation project that turned out to be more onerous than anticipated, and they decided to sell it. It is moored in the disused shipyard Jesper owns and from which he runs his company dealing in reclaimed building materials. It is centrally located, only a 15-minute bike ride from the centre of town, and moored alongside other houseboats in a neighbourly community. The owners canoe and swim in the sheltered waters and share an open sunny aspect over the Copenhagen waterfront.

Originally a Dutch boat, it had arrived in Denmark during the 1950s. Jesper purchased it seven years ago but the work is still ongoing. His plan was to renovate the hull, then re-build and re-furnish the living quarters, utilising as many previously used materials as possible from his yard. The pieces themselves would inform his design decisions. Some are new, such as the large square double-glazed windows – surplus stock due to a slight mis-measurement on site but perfect for the boat Jesper could build around them – while others are reclaimed and recycled. The floor was formerly in a sports arena but has been cut down to size and re-laid in a long herringbone pattern.

The serious and expensive structural repairs to the hull have been completed, as has a separate apartment in the bow section, but the main living section of the boat is a work in progress. It can be difficult to construct a stylish living area on top of a traditional boat hull – the solution in many cases is a simple boxed-shaped section. However, Jesper has broken the mould and created something more evocative and curvy, which is reminiscent of nature, the wind and the waves. The roof profile follows the curve of the hull and, with a sweeping overhang at the bow to soften the shape, it looks simple and elegant – it doesn't shout.

copenhagen recycled boat

style notes

This is a boat that is not minimally furnished or decorated but it has created a balance between the exterior (the magnificent location, the light, the water and the landscape) and an interior that is beautiful yet thrifty and comfortable. Neither overwhelms the other.

Jesper knew that flooding the interior with the characteristic Scandinavian soft light would be a challenge, especially in the darker hull section that was punctuated by only a few portholes. Using reclaimed building materials, he has maximised the light penetration in the bedroom, bathroom and kitchen areas with large windows and even a glass floor. And by furnishing the boat with vintage pieces, Jesper and Jette have created a very comfortable living space – a mix of vintage designer and distressed industrial chic.

All the walls are painted white, with areas of vertical wooden panelling created from cutting up reclaimed doors that were not usable in their own right. The decorative textured surface runs from down below up through the ladder-way to the upper sitting room and is visible through the glass floor. The fabric colours are bright but flat, with matt felt-type wools, but apart from the blue textured-wool 1950s sofa bought in a Swedish auction, all the other textures are found within the building materials themselves.

The narrow-runged, red-oxide worn metal ladder is a piece that is usually used as a part of scaffolding. The lengths were not quite long enough, so Jesper welded two sections together to obtain the correct length. With another nod to industrial ship design, he has set the bottom of all the doors about 10cm (4in) off the ground, as on a naval vessel or submarine. The stunning internal doors to the bedroom were rescued from an old military boat. Labelled 'torpedum', they have a beautiful green distressed surface, heavy riveted edges and levered and secure fastenings – they're a central feature.

The two 1950s kitchen units are utilitarian in style and painted in the same muted flat tones as the dining chairs and the textiles in the sitting room and kitchen diner. The lamps and decorative small objects add even more colour and sculptural elements to the space, and they reflect Jette's affinity for form and colour. She used to work as a glass blower and scoured flea markets and auction houses to source exactly the right pieces for the boat. Meanwhile, Jesper's love of reusing building materials to add light, patina and texture has made them both recognise that mixing furnishings with decorative pieces and bright, flat-coloured textiles is a recipe for success.

berlin yoga boat

Imke Wagerin nicknamed her boat the *African Queen* after the vessel in the classic movie. Its exact history is unknown, but it was probably built, less romantically, in the 1920s to transport coal. Imke bought it in 2007, initially as her home but now as a base for her yoga and coaching work and for rental holiday accommodation. Buying the boat was part of Imke's decision to change her career and embrace a more holistic lifestyle change. A former journalist, she wanted a more relaxed and considered work-life balance and the boat symbolised her new start.

However charming and evocative the boat looked, it had a less than illustrious past. It had previously been sunk and it reeked of spilled engine oil. And just after Imke completed the renovation work and moved in, she had a phone call to say it was sinking again – with her cat on board! She rushed back to find 40 firemen pumping it out and trying to stabilise it. Although the cat was rescued, the boat had listed badly. The cause of the sinking was attributed to it being too tightly attached to its moorings, which, when combined with rising levels in the river, had led to the low-mounted portholes taking on water. Luckily, Imke's family and friends all rallied round to help dry out her personal belongings and photographs and to wash and dry her clothes. However, despite this, collectively they urged her to get rid of the boat, arguing that it was neither safe nor financially viable as a project and that she should start afresh elsewhere.

This would be enough to put most people off, but Imke wasn't deterred. She had good vibes about the old boat and she was determined to live on it. She hired a team of builders to rectify the problems, rebalance the ballast, make the mooring more flexible and stabilise the hull. Three months later, she moved back in. As she says: 'If you want to make your dreams come true, you have to go look and make them happen.'

style notes

Imke's belief in this delicate old boat, her love of yoga and healing and her determination to make this craft habitable led to her placing a Buddha statue in a sunny spot inside a window. His kindly and watchful gaze into the boat's interior was reassuring and comforting. Upstairs the sitting/coaching/yoga room is bright and airy with two big skylights, windows and a glass door to a small outside deck area. The space has a radiance and is very uplifting. There's also a kitchen area, bathroom and office/thinking space, which leads to another deck at the bow. Down below are a large bedroom and a utility area.

The boat is furnished very simply. Painted white throughout, the furniture consists of a few vintage pieces. The glamorous and heavily ornate oval-framed portrait of a Sophia Loren-style woman came from a local house clearance. The gold-edged 1950s crockery and coffee pots were bought at a flea market, and the desk in Imke's office was from her childhood home. Some of the artefacts, such as the menorah, hail from her time working on a kibbutz. Some features are the original ones, including the kitchen and office cupboards, and the sliding doors to the office and bathroom with their 1920s art nouveau feel.

Imke is a courageous soul. When the boat sank, most people would have given up, but she pushed ahead regardless. You look outwards to the river, enjoy the light and feel as if you are in 'another' world. The vibrant city of Berlin is right outside on your doorstep, but the spirit and style of this old boat transports you to a very quiet, tranquil space.

For young couples setting out on life's journey together, there are always challenges. Living on a small boat makes demands on both partners, but, as Sophie says, 'If you can survive on a 10m (35ft) boat, you are set up for life'. The couple started out living together on such a small boat. Sophie was an art student in Scotland at the time while Kendall was working a few hundred miles away in London. They were always apart and realised that one of them would have to make the move to be with the other. One day, Sophie said, half-jokingly, 'If you find us a boat to live on, I'll come to London', so Kendall did. It made sense: they had a limited budget and Sophie longed for a simpler lifestyle with less stuff. She wanted to shed her belongings and start again. She had been a hoarder of fabrics, books and artworks, but she moved down to London with just three small boxes. This was her opportunity to de-clutter and start afresh in a new city. Drawn to small interesting spaces that are out of the ordinary, Sophie would 'rather live in a beautiful shed than a horrible flat' and things began to fall into place.

Sophie and Kendall's relationship survived and flourished in the small space and they took to life on the water, so much so that eventually they purchased a bigger boat. *Defiance* is 17.4m (57ft) long, 10 years old and sited on a secure central London mooring. They were cautious and had it lifted out of the water for a survey in a dry dock, but the metal hull and superstructure were in good condition. Although it's cheaper to buy a boat than a bricks and mortar property, you also have to set money aside for maintenance and improvement, which the couple sensibly did. Neither had any knowledge of boat-owning, but they were eager to learn and knew that it is only by being put into a situation that you can begin to figure things out.

sophie and kendall

style notes

Once the boat was theirs, Sophie and Kendall had to transform it into their home. The previous owner had painted the interior almost entirely in gloss red paint above the gunnels and grey below, so the couple borrowed an electric sander, and many hours and several coats of paint later, it started to feel more homely. Some of Sophie's belongings had survived her 'moving to the city' cull. The couple enjoy cooking and a set of French 1930s copper pans, purchased in Spitalfields market, hang from the kitchen ceiling. In time, they plan to replace the red kitchen sink and counter. The sitting room is decorated with art – paper cuts of Sophie's along with other pieces collected along the way.

This couple likes to change things around, so they prefer the flexibility of freestanding furniture. A friend who is a set dresser donated the fruit and wine boxes that are used as bookshelves. A fan of William Morris, Sophie purchased some fabric on eBay to make the tiny sets of curtains for the porthole windows, while the curtain at the main door for keeping out draughts of chilly air is an old well-loved throw. Sophie realises that you have to be diligent about what you buy for life on a boat – the available space has to be thought about carefully. Her books, art, plants and Kendall cooking make her feel at home, but all

the everyday items need to have character and add creative value rather than just exist. Also, 'not having much storage space is a blessing as well as a curse'.

It's customary on this mooring for the owners to decorate the small piece of land directly opposite their boat on the other side of the towpath as a way to make the space attractive and pleasant for everyone, a gesture of communal appreciation. Sophie and Kendall have done this in a collaborative way with their neighbour by building a small wooden deck area, just big enough for a table and chairs, and by decorating the small tree with lights and old baubles hanging on vintage ribbons. When the weather is kind, Sophie works outside here, drawing and painting at the table.

Their unusual new home has become a magnet for their friends, too, who love to visit and experience the shared sense of community. One of the neighbouring boats runs a supper club, there are walks along the towpath and it's relaxing just to spend some time by the water or messing about in boats. Although it's relatively small, this boat, its environment and the people who live there all combine and complement each other to create a very social and appealing space.

australian sailing boat

When Sophie Thé found a job as a steward on a superyacht, she anticipated that the work would take her to some exciting new places. What she didn't realise, however, was that it might give her career a totally new direction. In between looking after her passengers and doing her everyday chores, she found an outlet for her creativity by making subtle alterations to the vessel's interior design. 'Styling was something I found myself practising instinctively on the yacht, on a daily basis, as a way of relieving the monotony of the work. It became my second nature,' she explains.

Seven years later, in 2001, Sophie left her job to study interior design and soon gravitated towards professional styling. However, she didn't leave life on the waves behind her – her partner, Australian landscaper Niki Baillie-Jackson, found a beautiful 1960s sailing boat for sale online. The 11m (36ft) ketch, named *Gwenn A Du*, boasted a cheerful creamy hull and an interior of exposed New Caledonian kauri timber.

Niki was smitten. He had just spent some time in laid-back Laos and he wasn't ready to re-join the Sydney rat race – boat life offered a perfect compromise. Despite zero experience on the water, he soon learnt how to handle and, just as importantly, maintain *Gwenn*. It was a steep learning curve of painting and varnishing, salting the decks after rain and airing the boat in warm weather. He was rewarded for his efforts with a tranquil refuge away from the hustle and bustle of the city and a romantic one at that – with dinners of home-cooked bouillabaisse and a glass of Côtes du Rhône out on deck under the stars.

style notes

With so much travel behind them, it is not surprising that the boat's interior reflects Niki's and Sophie's nomadic tendencies. Small nautical souvenirs, from a piece of dried coral to a vintage admiral's uniform, have been lovingly curated in the living area in a low-key way. The overall effect is loose and autobiographical, but it's underpinned by practical seamanship. This boat functions at anchor and at sea, and any clutter would get in the way.

The personal effects and domestic necessities on display are framed by the rich timber of the hull's interior. The wood has a strong, warm tone, which could easily overpower the confined space, so it's punctuated by blocks of bright white paint on some of the walls and behind the dining table. This is not only a great way of enhancing the sense of space but it also ensures that the fabric detailing of the soft furnishings, especially the exquisite teal design on the bench upholstery, is given a lift.

Sophie's French upbringing is evident throughout. She favours bold statement pieces, such as draping a fading tricolor above the entrance to the bedroom. It's a stark contrast to the prettily patterned ensigns fluttering from the masts outside, which give the boat an inviting, bohemian appearance. These unorthodox pennants are so important to the philosophy that Sophie and Niki share afloat. 'Through work I've been lucky enough to see the most beautiful houses around the world, the most expensive atmospheres money can buy,' Sophie explains, 'but for me nothing is as beautiful as living on a boat. I feel like a queen on *Gwenn*.' By flying the flag for independence, simplicity and bucketloads of creativity, the couple's boat truly becomes their castle.

prague houseboat

Most of us want to live in a beautiful place, and doing your best to achieve this can demand a creative and inventive solution. For some people, a simple houseboat on a city river is the fulfillment of that dream, but it often involves an element of compromise. The architects of this project describe it as a process of finding 'the best value ratio' of flexibility and asking yourself these key questions: 'How do I want to live today?' and 'How shall I live in two years' or 10 years' time?' We all need to recognise that things in our lives will change, and it is only by analysing our situation and long-term goals that we can find a place that is beautiful and works for us.

The owner of this houseboat in Prague works in the hospitality industry and wanted to live somewhere peaceful and beautiful. He purchased a half-sinking, run-down boat and set about repairing, re-designing and rebuilding it to create a restful space that made maximum use of the location and the light. Like Prague's recent political history, life has changed for houseboat dwellers. Perceived as a sanctuary of relative freedom in the communist era when they were used as weekend houses, the boats were individually built by their owners, which made them enormously diverse in their design, but in 1967 houseboats were prohibited and many were moved out of the water to be used as land-based cottages instead. Over the subsequent years, however, the boats re-emerged on the rivers, and this one had seen better days.

The new owner wanted to reconstruct this old houseboat, which is moored on a riverbank in the centre of Prague. His dream was to live in the heart of the city, so he could work close by, socialise with friends, live on the water and embrace the small joys of city life, such as the Sunday farmers' market on the central quay.

style notes

The simplicity of its shape is intrinsic to this boat's beauty. It has the essence of a cabin – a humble, simple and honest structure, which appeals to our homely and unassuming sentiments. The ideal of a homestead runs deep. The existing property, built in the 1980s, needed urgent work to prevent it sinking because the pontoon base on which it sat was half submerged. The budget for redesigning the boat was very tight, so a realistic assessment had to be made as to where the money could most sensibly be spent and what compromises would have to be made. Fortunately, the owner has a friend who is a carpenter, so the quality of the work was not an issue. He lived onboard for six months while he worked on the construction and refurbishment.

The pontoon was rebuilt and the main structure was made 1m (3ft) wider than the original, while retaining its shape. The interior of the boat required the most work – it was unattractive as well as outdated. It's a small space and the design needed to be simple and effective. Adding several new windows let in more light, making the space appear much larger. The exterior is clad in larch, which is well suited to the local climatic conditions, while the interior is lined with spruce. The architects have deliberately adopted a simple approach, so you can see, at a

glance, how the boat is constructed. The surface elements have been left visible, as has the electrical cabling. It is an honest space and, as they say, 'Truthfulness is one of the basic tenets of our design'.

Although it is compact, the interior feels remarkably spacious and airy, with the best qualities of luminosity and sensitive design detail. For instance, the dark wooden floors, which are painted and varnished, beautifully highlight the warmth and patina of the lighter wooden walls, with their single layer of white varnish. And the dark outline of the shelves adds a striking graphic detail. The houseboat sits on a larger pontoon, which extends like a deck out onto the water. Glazed doors open to the front and a glazed section above, reaching right up into the apex, increases the reflected light within. Contrasting light and darkness invade this space – the dark water outside seems to flow right into it, making the building an extension of its natural environment.

This small simple space is a floating urban cabin, which has been designed and built with consummate care. And while you can use it to enjoy everything that city life has to offer, it is still, essentially, a place of dreams.

businesses

Setting up our own business is a dream for many of us, and this chapter looks at some examples where folk have wanted to do just that but have stepped outside the usual norms to make their dreams a reality. Although the path does not always run smoothly, creating and recognising our own opportunities and looking at life and work from a different perspective have been key to the achievements of the projects in this chapter.

For several of the boat owners featured, the affordability and flexibility of location that a boat offers has given them an advantage over a conventional land-based business. *Word on the Water*, a London-based, second-hand bookshop on a barge on a canal, serves office workers on their lunchtime breaks as well as travellers and commuters from the adjacent busy train terminus.

Multi-functioning living and business space, too, are evident on *The Book Barge*, a narrow boat that houses a new and vintage bookshop but which is also home to Sarah Henshaw. Her taste is impeccable – as are her standards of housekeeping and tidiness – and the style of her books, displayed on tables and vintage chairs in the context of a fully lived everyday life, is enlightened.

Not that it's all literary – it's good to party, too. *Disco Volante* is a cocktail bar boat specialising in the owner's handcrafted bespoke vodka. There is a functioning still on board, and the floating cinema cruises the canals of East London serving up art, either on board or projected onto the side of the boat.

And if dinner is more to your taste than cocktails, a ferryboat in Amsterdam has been converted into a floating restaurant. Its industrial design and tough materials have been integrated into a modern textural space with an open deck where you might have driven your car on board in its previous existence.

Starting and running any business takes courage, and all these people have found a way to take that leap into the unknown. These are exciting and surprising projects that have set them on their path to fulfilling their dreams.

the book barge

We've all been there. To get what you want in life inevitably involves compromise, facing up to reality and finding solutions to problems. Sarah Henshaw is no exception. She runs *The Book Barge*, a bookshop on a canal boat, which manages to combine super-stylish small space living with a flourishing business.

Sarah was an entertainment journalist, but she didn't relish city life. Moving back home to the Midlands, she considered looking for a job in local journalism until one day she had a flash of inspiration while sitting beside a canal boat marina. How about opening a shop on a boat selling classic, contemporary and children's books? Not necessarily heavily discounted bestsellers but an eclectic selection curated by herself? A bookshop she could move between different locations, from the local small towns to the larger cities of London, Manchester and Birmingham?

The idea took root and six months later she bought a boat. The first one she looked at, it's a traditionally designed 2006 narrow boat, which had been partially restored, by the previous owner, an electrician. The interior was almost ready to go and, with the help of Stu, her carpenter boyfriend, Sarah added a wooden floor and fitted bookshelves wherever she could, literally building her shop and starting her business.

Over time, her plans developed and the couple purchased a small run-down property in rural France, with a canal at the end of the garden, their intention to live on the barge while renovating the house. In order to achieve that dream and the next stage in their lives together, they decided to live on *The Book Barge*, saving every penny they would otherwise have spent on rent, while Stu kept on working and Sarah ran her business. So here we are...

style notes

Although the boat has two separate functions, Sarah has designed the space to look and feel like a whole. It is a very contemporary bookshop, with the vintage and modern books displayed as part of life. Artfully placed on a central table with the cookbooks in the kitchen area, the small book-shelved areas act as steps along the gunnels. The domestic and business aspects of the space work perfectly together – you don't feel as though you are intruding into a private space, nor living in a shop.

A careful choice of furniture (their bed is a 1970s double sofabed) keeps the interior extremely tidy. All the everyday living items have something to offer visually to the overall scheme, and colour plays its part in making this happen. The kitchen is painted yellow and grey. The square retro sink is from an old school and was purchased online. The fridge is a retro caravan model, with the door painted orange (inspired by the vintage anglepoise lamp beside the sink), and cutlery is stored in a space-saving narrow wooden cigar mould. The cups hang from travel-friendly hooks. These are all practical yet stylish solutions to a moving, floating small-space, multi-purpose home.

However, despite the limited space, it isn't all set aside for practicality. A metal IKEA storage rack has been customised with a plywood back and houses some of Sarah's collection of typewriters, all in working order. Look even more closely – joy and

companionship haven't lost out to practicality either. The whole kitchen unit has been built to include a home for Napoleon Bunnypart, Sarah's beloved pet rabbit. Hardly a space-saving essential, but what's life worth without a pet?

A wood-burning stove sits on a slate hearth within a surround of 1970s vintage tiles. A row of sharp yellow oblong tiles adds a modern aspect to the overall look. The long central book table and benches were custom-made by Stu, using cast-off staircase newel posts for the legs. The top slides open to add another layer of display/storage.

The second bed space at the end of the boat provides the only area of relative privacy as well as storage space. It was made from unfinished OSB board with the manufacturing lettering left on show, as inspired by old tea chests. Beneath the bed are some handy built-in storage boxes. A small bathroom and further clothes storage are hidden from everyday sight behind small doors on either side at the back of the boat. The doors open and fasten together to create a small separate bathroom space.

Outside, a small table and chairs are used for dining or as an additional book display area in good weather, and Sarah grows flowers, fresh herbs and edible leaves in a small planter at the stern of the boat. This is an example of beautiful, inexpensive, stylish and well thought-out design. It manages to be an effortlessly unselfconscious practical and private living space – and it's a great way to travel on life's journey.

Vodka and Poland are the two major players in this story, woven together by William Borrell, the entrepreneurial and hard-working owner of *Disco Volante*. It was named after the boat in Ian Fleming's novel *Thunderball*. The name means 'flying saucer' in Italian, an irony not lost on William given its ultra-slow travelling speed of 4.8 kph (3 mph). *Disco Volante* was built in the industrial shipyards of Gdansk, then shipped to Doncaster as part of a job lot. It was purchased by William as a shell and needed a major refit, starting from scratch. His plan was to transform the boat into a home for himself, so he could live affordably in central London, which he did for several years.

Over 20 years ago his family bought some land in northern Poland and started producing specialist unfiltered vodka. In the past, vodka had as much individual identity as whisky, brandy or cognac. Made in a low-tech, industrial way, like wine, its character changed from year to year. An idea gradually evolved, combining William's knowledge and skill as a bespoke vodka maker with his ownership of a tiny space in London's inner city urban landscape. He decided to turn his home into a business and set about obtaining a licence for the boat to sell alcohol, so he could showcase his vodka and invite bartenders to taste the different vintages. Although it was a long-winded process, he managed to obtain the only licence given to a floating distillery.

As with all good ideas, word quickly spread and two months into this new venture private bookings started flowing in. William even started to run daily canal boat cocktail cruises. He now employs three full-time staff: a bartender, a skipper and a maintenance man. *Disco Volante* has, in William's words, 'been re-born in year one'.

disco volante

style notes

Creating a sense of space is always a priority on narrow canal boats. This one, measuring 14m (45ft) with an average 2.7m (9ft) in the beam, has just enough headroom, while the etched windows along both sides and round wall-mounted mirrors help to reflect the light. There are also hatches and small open decks at each end. The main space is open plan, with a narrow corridor leading past a small bathroom to a bar section at the rear of the boat. In addition, William has lined the interior in light-reflecting, warm-toned maple wood, turning the sheets of wood to set the grain vertically and thereby produce the illusion of even greater height.

The main sitting/living/cocktail area of the boat has built-in sofas on each side beside a wood-burning stove and opens out onto the decks and roof area. The middle section has a counter and is dedicated as his work area. Sitting on the counter is his own vodka distillery. Delicate glass flasks and tubes distill his special brew and tell the story of what this boat is all about. Off a narrow corridor runs a small bathroom, and at the stern is the former bedroom. William has stripped away the signs of the boat's domestic past and removed the corridor wall to make the bar. Wallpapered in Vivienne Westwood wallpaper, it has a rock and roll edge. The bar is wooden palette fronted with the vodka is displayed in vintage wooden crates fixed to the walls as shelves.

The boat will shortly undergo another renovation – the bathroom will be re-sited and a dance floor added. From being William's home, it is now his business, not only promoting his brand of vodka but also a cocktail bar venue in its own right. The story is unlikely to stop here.

floating cinema

Less of a drive-in and more a potential dive-in, London's unique floating cinema was launched in 2013 to serve and unite local communities across the east of the city. The idea was first piloted in the run-up to the 2012 London Olympic Games, and it proved to be such a success that an 18m (60ft) barge was custom-made at Turks Shipyard in the historic docks in Chatham, Kent, to give the project a more permanent life on the water.

The screening programme is an art-meets-film mix of talks and shorts, with guests either seated in the onboard cinema auditorium, or treated to an outdoor towpath viewing, which can accommodate as many as 500 people. After the screenings, the boat chugs on to its next port of call, powered by a hybrid marine engine system that runs on eco-friendly bio fuel.

style notes

The style story behind the floating cinema is an unusual one. In June 2012 an open international design competition was launched, inviting architects from across the globe to submit their vision of what the picture house should look like. Duggan Morris Architects won, with a concept called 'A Strange Cargo of Extra-Ordinary Objects'. It drew heavily on the rich industrial heritage of the Lea Valley – the cinema's principal cruising route – and featured two main installations, which sit above the waterline on the base vessel, connected by a central terrace deck. This leads cinema-goers from the skipper's cabin to a finely crafted semi-translucent box, which is illuminated from within. This larger 'cargo' forms the cinema auditorium, containing rows of simple white seating. When movies play, heavy red curtains are drawn back in front of an attractive window lattice detail and you're transported, in every sense, as the opening credits begin to roll.

the floating allotment barge

Many of us who live in cities strive to engender a sense of community and achieve some outdoor space. Whether it's a tiny herb garden or a pretty window box, we try to create opportunities for engaging with nature. In this developing area of East London, the iron gate and entry-phone on a busy main road give no clues to what lies behind, but if you venture through the modern deluxe apartment block you'll discover a section of London's old industrial canal system.

This regeneration area is in constant flux, changing almost weekly, and the surrounding area, which was once entirely made up of Victorian warehouses and timber yards, has witnessed massive changes in recent years. Some of the striking old industrial buildings have been renovated and stand incongruously between the smart glass balconies of desirable modern urban residences. Meanwhile, the water has created its own established community, run by the not-for-profit Canals in Hackney Users Group. In an area with a long history of philanthropic endeavours, an old Regents Canal 'Hopper' barge hull was donated by the then British Waterways in 2009 – 'Hopper' was a non-mechanical barge used on the slightly wider Regents Canal for transporting soil, rubbish and waste. The conversion was sponsored by Shoreditch Trust and Capital Growth. It was a visionary and very simple project – to design and produce a community garden where there is no land at all, on an old barge hull – and it offers us a remarkable lesson in creative thinking.

style notes

The allotment, on the redundant hull of a wide-beam barge, is 21m (70ft) long. Pebbles form a drainage layer and also act as ballast, while lower-quality soil and better-grade topsoil make up the growing layer. The surface area available for vegetable growing is approximately 15 x 3.6m (50 x 12ft). Planks of wood from an old pontoon have been re-used as a central pathway along the length of the boat, and the gardeners established compost bins onboard, bringing in a bag of worms to break down the compost and soil.

Unusually, these boat dwellers have the benefit of their own vegetable and fruit garden. Residents and volunteers tend a floating organic allotment and duck pen, and the produce is free for all to pick and share. They grow fruit trees, raspberries, strawberries, rhubarb, redcurrants, gooseberries, various herbs, artichokes, beans, squash, courgettes, lettuces, kale, rainbow chard, beetroot, celery, celeriac and, of course, duck eggs.

The seven Khaki Campbell ducks live in an enclosure at one end of the boat. During the day they enjoy a relatively natural and free life, rambling and floating around the basin. In the evening, a wooden ramp is lowered so they can gain access to their fox-proof home.

This is a peaceful and beautiful place, both in terms of the goodwill and intentions behind the project, and in its representation of what can be created, given generosity, human endeavour and a true sense of community.

The 25m (82ft) *Mirosa* was built in 1892 to carry hay, straw and timber between London and the coast. It's now the summer home of Peter and Sally. Peter's special relationship with the barge began back in the 1970s when house prices were sky high, so he bought the boat to live on for 11 months of the year and sail during the summer. When he purchased the *Mirosa* she was in a desperate state and the deck was so rotten you couldn't walk on it for fear of falling through. The renovation was a major project and took several years, during which time Peter and Sally lived on board 'covered in sawdust and dirt'.

Peter's plan was to get the *Mirosa* ready to race and he persuaded Blue Circle Cement to sponsor them – the company used the barge to entertain clients while Peter and Sally organised the catering and sailing. They lived on the barge full-time for 18 years but now retire to their house on land for the winter. During the summer, they still provide chartered day trips and special events to finance the barge's maintenance costs. The *Mirosa* is one of only three barges still sailing without an engine. It was designed to be sailed by a man and a boy, which seems incredible when you look at the extensive rigging; as Peter says, 'three miles (4.8 km) of rope and wire are required to rig a barge like this'.

thames sailing barge

style notes

The interior has an understated nostalgic elegance, and the original craftsmanship remains the predominant feature. The splendid woodburner takes precedence in the shiplapped saloon with built-in seating furnished in deep red cosy fabrics, echoing the traditional rusty red of the flax sails and creating a homely ambience. The cut-out prisms in the deck flood the interior with abundant light. The bulkheads house the *foc's'le* at one end, now the catering galley, and the *cabin aft* at the other end where the skipper and his mate once slept. The original wooden cupboard doors and bunks are steeped in history. Lit by a shaft of light through the hatch, the cabin has a restful, calm and magical atmosphere.

Most of the barge is constructed out of pitch pine, which is now virtually impossible to source. The mainhold is furnished with stuffed hessian sacks, providing snug seating for the crew, as well as bags of sails, waterproof coats, boots and copious amounts of rigging. Next to a wooden staircase is Peter's essential work bench, which is in constant use. Humble, steadfast, honourable and strong, he has devoted his life to caring for this incredible vessel, and with Sally's support, they are an inspiring team. The sense of unity and extended family spirit flow as gracefully as the elegant *Mirosa* continues to sail.

word on the water

We've all read about independent bookshops struggling to survive against the Internet giants, but here's an example of the business turning back to its roots. A curated selection of books, all second-hand copies, artfully displayed, affordably priced, the owners engaging in conversation with the office workers, travellers, canal walkers and tourists who make up the bulk of their customers. This is a first for me, too, seeing 'reverse customers' proudly giving the owners a copy of a recently finished, hardback pre-read book to sell on – it's added to the shelves moments later.

Word on the Water is moored just outside an exit from a busy London underground station. Three partners manage the 1920s Dutch barge bookshop, each with their own specialised role. There's the 'Captain', boat owner Noye, a Frenchman who manages the boat and creates its artful displays; the 'Doctor', people-person Paddy who also deals with the admin; and John, the 'Prof', who's worked in publishing for 22 years. As John says, 'None of us could have done it on our own – there's energy in our collaboration'. They each bring different skills and attributes, but all three of them love the water and live on boats. They met and became friends within the boat community and live nearby, often walking down the canal towpath to work.

This rather glamorous boat was formerly home to Noye and his family in France. His original plan was to ship it to London in a container with the intention of selling it but, fortunately, there were no takers and the boat's still here. And, as John describes their business: 'We take pride in every aspect of selling the books we've chosen; we've had people walk in here and burst into tears at finding a copy they've been seeking for years... Everything doesn't have to be the same as everything else.'

MIND YOUR HEAD!

style notes

Outside, it can be hard from certain angles to see the boat beneath the neatly piled and laid-out rows of books, stacked in different levels, lined up attractively overlapping each other, most of their covers facing forwards. Displayed in wooden crates, on long wooden planks, or in old plastic bread delivery trays, the books make a rich tapestry, a creative and artful shop window that begs to be looked at and pondered over. On top of the boat there's a small performance space where, on summer evenings, jazz musicians play. An awning provides shelter to enable trading in all weathers.

Inside, the boat is divided into three sections: all low-ceilinged and leading into another, each is like a comfortable, cosy sitting room. The book selections are themed for each room: children's; mind, body and spirit; and classics. The titles aren't filed alphabetically by author but 'more in order of how long we have had them'. Bookshelves fill the space from floor to ceiling and wall to wall. They were created from old wardrobes with their doors removed, pieces of original furniture, wooden crates and shelves made of scaffold planks, all stained the same colour as the floorboards. Among them are comfortable well-worn leather chairs, a pile of flattened seat cushions and a built-in sofa with kelim throws and cushions.

A wood-burning stove provides warmth, while the scent of joss sticks wafting out of the open window onto the towpath attracts passing customers.

The boys have created a unique environment here, which is way beyond just a bookshop. This is its own world with its own life. Understanding the aesthetic is easy when Paddy tells me that 'it feels like the twelfth-century thatched country cottage in which I was brought up'. It does, indeed, feel like home and you want to spend time here – pick a book off the shelf, sit down and read all afternoon.

Even the open stern area of the boat feels like a sitting room. Star the dog lies on the worn cream leather banquette sofa beside a simple bio ethanol outdoor fireplace, and there's a red well-worn leather library chair and bookshelves built all around. Even a temporary roof covering has been installed, on which sit the two solar panels that power the lights and music.

The character of the original boat isn't lost, but it's an entirely creative re-interpretation of it, like an artisan travelling marketplace, which draws people in not only to look but also to step on board, chat, sit down and read. And rather than this being a personal space, it's an environment to be shared by everyone.

Pont 13 is a lucky little number. From scrap metal to one of the hippest culinary haunts in Amsterdam, the boat's strange journey is a salvage and creative triumph. Formerly a ferry across the IJ lake in northern Amsterdam, it was decommissioned at the end of the 1990s after nearly 70 years in service. No more tearful farewells on the gangplank nor excited footsteps pacing the deck on arrival into port; the vessel's fate hung in the balance as her owners tried to flog the hull for used iron.

But her story wasn't quite over yet. René Langendijk looked beyond the rust tears and inevitable renovation costs to visualise a bar-restaurant moored in trendy Haparandadam, where the port ends and the city begins. It opened in 2005 serving a winning mix of 'slow food' cuisine and sensitive design, and the eatery continues to be a popular dining choice for tourists as well as locals. While feasting on house favourites, customers can enjoy the impressive Amsterdam harbour skyline and be lulled by the chimes from yacht halyards bobbing alongside. How many other top restaurants accommodate moorings for hungry sailors?

Other quirks include a St Bernard dog called Storm and utilitarian all-weather plastic-protected menu clipboards à table. All this in a ship that wears its heritage so loosely that diners can still marvel at the beams, like a rib cage wrapping around the domed ceiling of this leviathan dining vessel and the post-industrial waterfront, where it's not uncommon to find students living in revamped shipping containers. This space has a timeless quality and a make-do mentality, both hewn from materials that were built to last.

pont 13

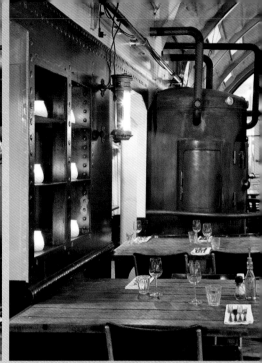

style notes

Pont 13 is the ultimate salvage success story, with a little bit of steam punk thrown in for good measure. Little effort has been made to disguise the original architecture, including the imposing engine chamber, which makes up the enormous metal heart of the dining area. From it, various pipes wave skywards like giant octopus arms before sucking the wall into their grasp. The old wooden floorboards are worn by decades of foot passengers, while rivets pockmark the satin sheen of the metal walls. This is not contrived industrial chic – this space has been carved from what was there before. Colour is applied cleverly, highlighting the odd shapes and complicated forms that make up a commercial ship build. Dark Oxford blue is wrapped around the creamy biscuit of the upper walls and beamed ceiling before meeting a green, domed roof, which curls like a huge wave over the room.

'Bricks' of natural light rain down on the dark tabletops, thrown from rectangular windows carved out of the roof panels. The glass entranceway and halo of side windows keep the restaurant surprisingly bright. At night, traditional-style nautical wall lights are a beacon to the boat's commercial past.

Spaces like this work well because they capture the memories and materials of a bygone age while also looking forward. The honest and sensitive approach to structure and space is inspirational and makes for wonderfully timeless architecture. This restaurant design isn't just flavour of the month – it will continue to serve up a visual treat for many years to come.

sealander

Caravanning on the shores of a tranquil lake is many people's idea of a perfect summer getaway, but what if you could tow your trailer straight into the water too? That's the simple genius behind the *Sealander*, an amphibious caravan that lets holidaymakers switch seamlessly between a mobile home and messing about on the water. On land, it's pulled by a standard towbar but afloat it assumes all the characteristics of a powered boat, with a long-pin outboard motor, which also runs the on-board appliances.

A roadworthy houseboat isn't a new idea. There's delightful black-and-white Pathé footage from the golden age of caravanning in the 1960s, showing the amphibious *Creighton Gull* chugging along the River Thames at Henley with open sunroof, four beds, a kitchen and discreet closet for a portable toilet. What sets the *Sealander* apart, however, is its more obviously aspirational yacht-informed appearance. It took creator Daniel Straub two years to design, build and test, but he's satisfied that all the hard work has paid off, commenting that it 'extends the possibilities of camping and leisure'.

style notes

Inside there's an exciting fusion of traditional and modern materials. Clean stainless steel and plastic lines lie comfortably against nautical wooden textures and leather upholstery. A sunroof and large windows on either side flood the space with light. Space is maximised through multi-functional furniture – the benches convert into two beds. For the chassis, fibreglass-reinforced plastic mats are fused into a seamless whole and sealed with a gel coat, giving a gleaming finish. To transform it from a camper into a boat, you just attach the outboard motor to the stern and launch it into the water – nothing could be simpler.

modernist

These modern responses to spending time living and working on the water are purpose-built and purpose-designed specific builds with ethical and aesthetic requirements and manifestos. Looking at their commonality, the one key factor is their relationship with the water, whether it's the functionality of the water itself – the floating Passivhaus Autarkhome uses the filtered and treated river water for all domestic purposes, including bathing, washing and drinking – or the boat's architectural relationship with the water – the Berlin houseboat has a huge wall of glass facing towards the open water.

Stylistically and decoratively, the finishes used are visually strong but coherent and simple. The Finnish floating office has a detailed modern filigree metalwork finish that is part decorative and part functional to allow the utilities behind to be adequately ventilated, while the Watervilla is inspired 'more by the curves of a Porsche than a caravan' but with a fully glass wall facing the water. The curves and smooth sleek structure of the boat itself are created from two strong sheets of corrosion-resistant aluminium permanently bonded to a thermoplastic core.

None of these floating builds have a motor – they are created on a pontoon and ballast-type construction and are definitely more in the vein of the gentle rocking of the water than having the ability to propel themselves. The design trend towards modernism – with its love of geometric forms, clean lines, attention to the materials used and the avoidance of decorative ornamentation – is clearly illustrated here.

All these boats are light in feeling as well as in luminosity. These are spaces that are more than just their physicality; they illustrate the best of good design and ecologically sound building ethics.

autarkhome

Designed to be completely off the grid, Pieter Kromwijk's floating Autarkhome is the first in a line of what he hopes will be many. With no demands on mains electricity, water or drainage, this home has untold potential for modern sustainable cities. The key principles follow the classic Passivhaus philosophy of super insulation, complete draft-proofing, roof-top solar panels, active waste water and drinking water systems, low-energy LED lighting and a structural design that provides shelter from direct sunlight in summer and harnesses all available ambient light in winter. The walls are 55cm (22in) thick with expanded polystyrene insulation; the glass windows and doors have the most efficient triple glazing available; and the ventilation system, powered by the solar panels and draft-proof structure, mean that even in the depths of the Dutch winter no heating is necessary.

The house is an independently functioning unit, and although this one floats, Pieter foresees the possibility of creating an amphibious version suitable for use on land or water as a response to climate change, and the increased risk of flooding. His approach to the design was to look at examples of how different communities function. He discovered that in Canada, large geographical distances meant that some isolated properties were already using modern, efficient and independent means of water, drainage and power supplies. From Pieter's perspective, this was 'putting the good things together in a good way'. By extracting the best ideas from these proven technologies and applying them to the build, he felt that he could create something that was just as innovative, attractive, practical and responsive to the challenges of climate change, increased risk of flooding, and changing energy costs and supply issues.

style notes

Pieter's initial training as a landscape architect had instilled in him the need to create a good sense of light and outside space. The Autarkhome has two large terraces: one upstairs off the main bedroom, which is sheltered by the solar panels on the roof extending above it; and the other a deck area over the water, which opens via a large glazed door and wall from the lower sitting area.

Upstairs all the bedrooms and the bathroom run off a single corridor, but down below is an open-plan big kitchen, dining and lounging area. Furnished as a concept by IKEA, it is simple and modern, with clean lines, featuring minimal detailing and modern materials.

The sustainable intentions of the building have not been overlooked and many of the interior materials, such as the grey ceramic floor tiling down below and

the dark grey stair and upstairs carpeting, apply the concept of C2C ('cradle to cradle') and are safe for people and the environment. Not only are they reusable and manufactured with renewable non-polluting energy but they also function in a way that advances social and environmental justice.

This isn't a family home yet, but that day is not far away – either as the ultimate 'lock up and leave' sustainable weekend retreat or a permanent dwelling on the water. It begs the question why these technologies are not more commonplace. The building looks and feels modern, spacious, light, clean and comfortable, a place where you would be happy to live. It speaks of a regard for the environment and, of course, treading as lightly as possible on the planet.

When offered a completely free hand to create a modern houseboat, the mind races with possibilities, so rich is our visual history, but this boat looks forwards in a very modern direction towards simplicity, restfulness and a sense of space and light. This project was initiated by Chris and Oliver Laugsch, the co-founding brothers of 'Welcome Beyond', a boutique vacation rental agency. For the design of the boat they looked to the Dutch architect Bertjan Diphoorn, whose company Flodd builds handcrafted and unique floating homes. With a love of geometry, using both the properties and finish of raw materials, and conveying the movement of the water as well as an aesthetic valuation of the surrounding natural habitat, they set about their task.

Located on Lake Rummelsburg, a small inlet on the River Spree in the eastern part of Berlin, it is 15 minutes' away from the city centre. Measuring 60 sq m (646 sq ft), the hand-built boat is principally rectangular in form and totally glass fronted. With its westerly aspect towards the water, it catches the summer sun, while in winter the glistening surface of the lake and soft milky light fill the space. Chris says that when 'the water is frozen and covered in snow, it has a really peaceful and fascinating atmosphere'.

Heated by a freestanding wood-burning stove, the large main living space is comforting and warm. The kitchen is open-plan, and a dividing wall, with a sliding door, separates the queen-size bedroom and adjoining bathroom with its dual washbasins and walk-in shower. A second double bed folds down from the living-room wall. The overall feeling is that of a retreat from the city – a quiet and peaceful space. And, of course, if a big boat passes or if it's a windy night, it will gently rock you to sleep, too.

berlin modern houseboat

style notes

Although essentially an urban houseboat, this is a luminous and uncluttered space. The grey, polished, poured concrete floor complements the local light, the creamy hues of the skyscape and the sheen on the water. The boat, sky and water are threaded together with this muted colour palette. Injecting some warmth is the patina of the pine-beamed ceiling – with an understated elegance, the beams run the entire length of the boat.

The smooth gleaming white surfaces of the kitchen units cut cleanly away from the concrete floor, and the diverse rich and raw materials are sensitively and thoughtfully assembled. There is no pattern or extraneous detail; all that matters is that each plays its part simply and cleanly. The cushions are rectangles of geometric colour punctuating the monochrome palette. The furniture and soft furnishings are an intrinsic part of the architecture as a whole, rather than an added afterthought to create another mood. Everything is considered – the details, the furniture and the cushions were all specially handmade, making this a space to be seen, lived in and felt as an entirety.

Exposed aluminum crossbeams help to emphasise the linear geometry of the space and draw attention to the surrounding cityscape. The beautifully sparse but panoramic views require little else except the hues of the changing skies. There is no competition here – nature and the light will win out. The wide wooden deck gives you the sense of not being hermetically sealed. At night, the twinkling lights of the city reflect on the water, and while you are blissfully removed from it you are simultaneously sewn into the fabric of the waterscape and are very much integral to the environment and the city.

What do you get if you cross a Porsche with a traditional Dutch houseboat? A piece of design brilliance, it transpires. The Watervilla de Omval is not a laughing matter, having been nominated for one of Holland's top architectural prizes, the Gouden AAP, in 2011. Built in 2010, it is the brainchild of Amsterdam-based +31Architects, whose client had demanded less 'caravan' and more German high-performance sports car in the style brief. They made a mood board for their vision, and the image that resonated most with their ideas was of a Porsche, an icon with beautiful curves.

Curves is what they got – the sleek houseboat rests on the Amstel River like the outstretched neck of a swan. 'When you see it, it seems obvious, but it took quite some effort to get there,' admits the architect Jorrit Houwert. 'It is one simple gesture that keeps everything together.' In fact, the finished line, made from two strong sheets of corrosion-resistant aluminium permanently bonded to a thermoplastic core, owes a lot to the restrictions imposed on the build from the start. Tasked with creating a double-storey floating house not exceeding the height restrictions of more than 3m (10ft) above water level, the design team initially struggled to accommodate an upper sun terrace. It was only when they altered the floor plan and created a split-level design that the solution – and the resultant shape – became obvious.

watervilla de omval

style notes

The boat's striking contour informs the interior furnishings, too. A white wall cabinet in the open-plan living room, which hides the television and sound system, was custom-built by a cabinetmaker to the same proportions as the exterior. These sculptural forms continue with the adjacent Frank Gehry Wiggle Side Chair.

However, the biggest inspiration was the water itself. The north-facing view of it is maximised by floor-to-ceiling windows opening out onto the river's wide bend. The orientation means that the natural light can be enjoyed without the houseboat heating up excessively, while the minimal framing around the glass deceives the eye into believing you are literally sitting on the water. It's a feeling that is enhanced by rendering the interior walls in bright white plaster and the absence,

wherever possible, of all visual barriers. Instead, subtle demarcations, such as a step into the kitchen, a roof light accent in the dining space and a focal fireplace drawing the eye in the living area, create zones of different functional uses. Within these is yet more multi-functionality. The long gas fireplace, for example, also disguises a window opening into a downstairs bedroom.

Despite the bold statements made by this houseboat, the designers are satisfied that it does not look out of place among its more traditional neighbours. Jorrit maintains: 'The boat has such a strong expression of its own, not only as an architectural form but also as a nautical one, that it could fit into every kind of environment. It could be moored on a waterway in a city – or even on the Amazon'.

netherlands home

'There is nothing – absolutely nothing – half so much worth doing as simply messing about in boats,' Ratty famously declares to Mole in Kenneth Grahame's waterways classic *The Wind in the Willows*. Wendy Alblas, her husband Jochem and their three children are equally enamoured with life afloat and can't get enough of it. As well as living on the water, they swim and sail after work, picnic on the grassy banks and even skate over the frozen canal in winter.

The family's houseboat is moored 20 minutes' away from Amsterdam on the delightful Nieuwe Wetering, a narrow canal dating back to the fifteenth century and connecting the rivers Amstel and Vecht. Wendy and Jochem were in their twenties when they left the bright lights of the city behind them and decided to settle here on a rather cramped traditional houseboat. When the children were born, the couple soon realised that they needed a bigger home and they moved up to a two-level vessel. Twelve years later, however, they had even bolder plans: to sell up and self-build a veritable ark for their growing family. They found a mooring with an attached strip of land that could accommodate a studio for Wendy, who was already a successful artist and now an amateur architect, too.

Her blueprint was realised by a local building firm specialising in houseboat projects. Accommodating a family of five was no easy brief, and extending the boat's width was restricted due to the narrowness of the waterway, but Wendy worked within these constraints to maximise the space with a deep concrete hull instead. If not exactly reaching Noah's biblical scale, Wendy's finished 'ark' nevertheless feels roomy and light.

style notes

On canvas, Wendy is known for her colourful, figurative compositions, but her interior design style is all about contrasting black and white surfaces and clean lines. This visual tension is diffused by the views of the natural contours and colours that flood in from outside through the vast floor-to-ceiling windows and two large skylights. In summer, the sliding glass doors open, and any boundary between the interior and exterior is blurred by the wooden floorboards, which extend out on to the spacious terrace.

In the kitchen, Wendy's obsession with eking out every extra centimetre possible from the design pays off. There's a flexible island around which the family cooks, eats and entertains. One of her paintings also serves up a welcome helping of colour.

A white palette dominates down below, where natural light is more difficult to source. The bedrooms peel off from a central bathroom, walled with rough wooden planks in the same brilliant white. Tongue-and-groove built-in cabinets with discreet finger pulls instead of obtrusive cupboard handles complement the unfussy design. It's a pleasing attention to detail and adds an informal touch to the basement level. This can be seen in the bedrooms, too, where mini plywood boxes shore up timber lengths to make desks, and cheerfully coloured plastic chairs exude an easy confidence. There are no timber floorboards down here. Instead, a polished concrete finish catches the light from the thin above-the-waterline windows to keep the scheme bright. It is also a practical choice for three adventurous children with muddy river banks in such close proximity.

A fleet of ice breakers might not be the obvious starting point for an office design, but when one of Finland's biggest shipping companies needed a new headquarters close to their ships, K2S Architects figured that a floating premises could be just the thing. Mikko Summanen, who helped lead this innovative project, explains: 'We sketched a few different versions on land first, but there was very little room. There were several benefits to a floating solution, including the possibility for the client to move operations to a different location in the future.'

That hasn't happened yet. The Arctia HQ still bobs adjacent to the black hulls of its towering icebreakers in front of the listed main building of the Finnish Ministry of Foreign Affairs in the heart of Helsinki. Far from being intimidated by the lofty neighbourhood, the floating office holds its own with an arresting perforated aluminium facade and sweeping timber-clad entrance hall. The build was largely carried out in a local shipyard, and precision and craftsmanship ooze from every corner of the 950 sq m (10,225 sq ft) construction. Floor-to-ceiling windows mean that the office workers can enjoy premium waterside views from their desks, and there's the added benefit of a novel new commute for some, with moorings for personal boats nearby.

So buoyed are K2S Architects by the success of this project that they're currently developing ideas for a floating school in Helsinki, as well as a waterways housing project.

finnish floating office

style notes

From afar, the Arctia HQ's exterior surface looks much like any other vessel in the harbour. Only close up is it possible to appreciate the corrugated sea of aluminium panels that clad its steel structure. Each one features scores of tiny perforations, abstract cross-shaped patterns inspired by ice crystals, snowflakes and traditional textiles worn by Finnish sailors. The beautiful fragility they add to the design is at odds with the powerful ice breakers looming behind. What's more, the perforations cleverly function as protective trellis for the technical installations behind which require ventilation.

The dichotomy continues in the boat's jaw-droppingly grand foyer. An orthogonal front desk made of black gunmetal steel holds aloft a model of an Arctia vessel in a glass case. In contrast, the geometry of the backdrop is softer with bright planks of Finnish pine bent around the lobby corners, using the same construction methods as those in traditional wooden sailing boats. The effect is both elegant and warming.

Behind this facade, the boat accommodates a variety of offices, workspaces, meeting rooms and a staff café. And in case you were wondering how tricky it might be delivering a PowerPoint presentation on the high seas, have no fear. The boat is stabilised by ballast tanks in each of the four corners of the building. These can be emptied or filled with water independently, allowing for levelling in different weather conditions.

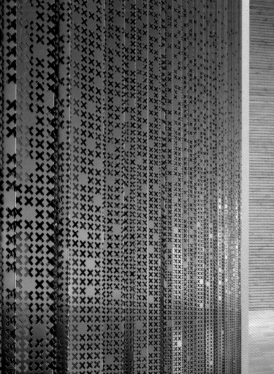

recycled

Starting with a 'previously used' vessel, all these homes have a base structure with a previous life. The boats have interesting narratives to tell: some were in commerce, like the Berlin grain transportation barge and the historic passenger ferry that brought new immigrants into New York City, while there are also oil rig escape pods and even a World War II German minesweeper. Their owners all looked way beyond conventional norms to the vessels themselves and considered how new life might be breathed into them for a quieter and often less dramatic use. Their achievements are astounding – they all thought outside the box in order to do something as extraordinary as this.

The ravages of decay, rust, leaks, and water take their toll here. For several of the owners, these are mammoth projects and they don't end with the full restoration. These are not easy beasts to keep afloat and the maintenance work is full-on. The owner of the Berlin barge likened his experience of the detailed repair and restoration of this great hulk of a boat in dry dock to analytical psychotherapy – so great were the hours spent, the manual labour stripping back years of paint, exposing the raw metal and rivets, and re-finishing it. And that was just making the boat a sound base on which to build his home, something that is an on-going project and part of his life.

The artist's recycled home, created from an old ferry, is barely recognisable in its original form, such is the layered, maximalist, beautiful collage of incongruous found materials that are stitched together, including an old coach, a caravan, a three-wheeler 'Robin Reliant' and a washing machine. And, of course, there's the minesweeper: a huge thing, purchased at modest cost, then moved to its mooring at enormous cost. It's a stunning piece of Cold War design, but how do you go about starting to create a home out of something so functional, practical and about as un-homely as you could imagine?

These intrepid owners are a brave bunch – creative, fearless, determined and hard-working. They are an inspiration to us all and I salute them.

berlin boat barge

Give any large space to a sculptor, and you know that it's not likely to end up looking like a conventional dwelling. For Brad Hwang, the on-going transformation of this boat into a family home is an evolving project. The *Odin* is a heavy-gauge, heavily-riveted steel boat – a hulking 30 x 4m (98 x 13ft) barge, built in 1892. Brad respects its industrial heritage and the lives of the boatmen who propelled it, punt-style, up and down the rivers and canals around Berlin. He came to live in the Mitte district in central Berlin in 1990. Living here gave him the artistic lifestyle he needed for his work, but the former edgy neighbourhoods became gentrified and their artistic communities priced out. The concept of space as a valuable commodity for investors and developers had an uncomfortable resonance, which made Brad think about the nature of space and its relationship with water, which you can't own and which is out of reach of speculators.

By chance, he met Ernst, who was seeking a creative purpose for the *Odin*, at that time a desolate rusting hull. Brad, with his artistic and practical hands-on talents, was the answer. Initially, he used it as a studio but later it became his home. Although he loves boat living, he is careful not to romanticise it. He says, 'it has clear disadvantages and less clear advantages – in the long term they balance each other out'. Wisely, along with his reverence for the boat itself, its past and the need to constantly maintain it, he has great respect for the water on which it floats: 'the water always wins'.

He thinks of the space as an on-going sculpture. Working with nature rather than against it, and respecting the past while being realistic and practical, have helped him to keep this beautiful beast of a boat afloat and to create a home within it.

style notes

Throwing out almost nothing, being careful about what he buys, using as many sustainable materials as possible, and recycling scrap materials have enabled Brad to give the boat a crafted individual feel and look. After years of work, imaginative and artistic endeavour, it's a three-bedroom family home carved out of a humble industrial barge. By looking at the possibilities, salvaging the overlooked and recognising that mass-produced doesn't have to dictate the terms of the spaces we inhabit, he has given this boat spirit.

Brad has an honest and sensitive approach to materials, structure and space and he has not attempted to conceal the original markings and rivets. The layering of expressive objects, colour and materials gives this boat a timeless quality as well as real warmth and substance – it is lived in and loved, an organic space that is constantly evolving.

Retaining the open-plan nature of the barge, he walled off a space for the bedrooms before refurbishing the main area of the interior as an open-plan kitchen, dining, sitting and play area. At the bow, a small bedroom opens up through metal hatch doors to the deck. The room is a challenging shape as there is not one straight edge or right angle, and each piece of material has to be fashioned to fit. They curve in two directions while an adjoining larger bedroom is still 'work in progress'. The living area is in the centre of the boat, while another bedroom and bathroom are in the old crew's quarters at the other end.

The space is currently top lit, apart from the entry hatches, and the roof structure incorporates the original loading bay lids. Some of these can be raised to act as windows whereas others are fixed in order to insulate the space. Around the edges are hinged wooden storage boxes, which can be used as seating, and the original floorboards have been re-sanded and re-laid. The wood-burning heating system runs at 93 per cent efficiency and heats the space through pipes laid into large clay wall tiles that emit a radiant heat. Brad sees the kitchen as a slight compromise. Within a constructed wooden frame, small IKEA drawer units house the regular kitchen equipment. The whole back wall can be removed to allow full access to the engine room behind.

Outside, on the riverbank, there's a wood store and a seating/dining/barbecue area, featuring a table made from an industrial cabling reel. The area is terraced, but attempts to grow vegetables have been thwarted by the poor sandy soil and the proliferation of local rabbits, which clear the crops before anyone else can get to them.

Above all, this is a family home. Although artful, it isn't self-conscious. It's practical and, as you might expect from a sculptor, spatially clever. The challenges of boat living continue: carving out and creating a changing space, not wasting materials, and making wise and considered decisions. Brad happily admits that 'we are still building, still living in a construction site...it never ends'. Nevertheless, this is a very happy place.

Where most people see junk and waste, Dutch maverick Denis Oudendijk sees architectural opportunity. He's one of four people behind the design laboratory REFUNC, a group committed to creating experimental structures from discarded objects with the motto: 'The world without a manual'. There's certainly nothing in the handbooks about how to turn an unwanted oil rig escape pod into a capsule hotel room, but that's what Denis did. The project came about as a by-product of another idea – a voyage around the European waterways by boat to find new audiences for the REFUNC way of thinking. The survival capsule seemed to be an ideal industrial craft for the trip, and when yet more were sourced, the project took a new turn.

Ultimately, he hopes to create a flotilla of guest rooms, but for now only a few are operational, including FAST (Free Architecture Surf Terrain), an experimental hostel and surf village in The Hague. Denis, who stayed in one for a month with his girlfriend, says they are the perfect way to see twenty-first-century life through new eyes. 'You can change a part of your world by looking in a different way at your surroundings. That's the whole idea with these rooms – to step out of the box and into the capsule.' They are also ideal for retreating from the stresses of modern daily life and spending some time alone. As Denis says, 'It's you and only you when you close the door'.

oil rig escape pods

style notes

Coloured vivid orange and measuring just 4.3m (14ft) in width, these capsules were originally manufactured as floating emergency vessels for oil workers on the rigs. They are definitely not lifeboats, and at the heart of their original design was the knowledge that their users would not be experienced seamen and might have only a very limited understanding of boats and the ocean.

When Denis got his hands on the escape pods, his priority was to change the interior as little as possible. 'Functionality can shift while design can stay the same', he explains, adding that this laissez-faire, low-energy approach to reinvention is in line with REFUNC philosophy. Naturally, the furnishings that have been added tell unique stories of their very different former lives. The giant hammock adorning one capsule, for example, was made from an old fishing net. A library filled with survival books and nautical manuals offers unusual bedtime reading, while authentic survival suitcases are filled with goodies to get guests through the night comfortably. The sheepskins on the floor and the sleeping bays add a splash of unexpected luxury, and in one pod the entire engine space has been removed to fit a standard bed.

ellis island ferry

The *Yankee* is a tough old ship, said to be the oldest ferryboat in the United States. She was built in 1907 and is registered as a historical vessel with the National Register of Historical Places. The 836 sq m (9000 sq ft) ferry navigated the waters between Maine's Calender Islands and Boston Harbor. During World Wars I and II she was enlisted as a patrol boat, but between them she returned to ferrying passengers, bringing immigrants from their incoming ships to be processed at Ellis Island prior to being granted entry to New York City.

In 1929 things changed again and she travelled between Battery Park, Liberty Island and Governors Island, carrying visitors to the Statue of Liberty. After World War II her steam engine was replaced with a diesel one and she returned to ferrying – from Providence Rhode Island to Block Island. This was the last chapter in her traditional working life, and retirement followed in 1983. She fell into disrepair as she lay rusted and neglected in a marine salvage yard. Her rescue came in 1990 when she was purchased, towed to Pier 25 in Tribeca, one of New York's hottest neighbourhoods, and an extensive restoration and conversion process began to save this symbolic fragment of the city's history.

Designers Victoria and Richard Mackenzie-Childs purchased the ferry in 2007 and continued the restoration. They wanted to keep her alive by using her as their home. They liked the space and felt that their artistic talents and practical ability could keep the old girl afloat. This journey was unlikely to be easy or painless, but they were keeping a piece of history afloat and being on the water, in proximity with the elements, with a sense of space around them, enabled them to 'live closer to nature than in an apartment'.

style notes

Until Hurricane Sandy stormed through the area, the ferry was moored at NYC's 100-year-old 12th St pier, but in July 2013 she was moved to her current location in South Red Hook, Brooklyn. During its stay in New York, Victoria built a 'Polka Dot Garden' of various vegetables growing out of 104 old truck tyres on the adjacent dock. The couple also raise their own chickens aboard the ferry, enjoying the daily fresh eggs they produce.

In keeping with the spirit of recycling and preservation, the ferry's most characteristic features were integrated – the passenger deck and a beautiful dining room. Even the helm is used as a cosy office space. The exterior is restored along classic lines and its history is there to be seen in the design, finish and materials. Inside, it's a similar story: the public areas retain their sense of permanence and quality in their original polished rich woods.

The private rooms tell a different narrative – more individualistic, densely layered and decorative in their painterly style. There are few surfaces that have not been decorated in this colourful riot of patchwork quilts, tartans, artisan ceramics, feathered fringes, stripes, painted floor cloths and paintings.

Richard and Victoria's latest dream is to turn the boat into a place where people and businesses can conduct meetings in the conference room and 'become immersed with the rock of the ship'. As they describe their achievement: 'Our natural talent is creating environments – we can't help it. We love the challenge of taking something cast aside and reusing it in new ways. Nobody comes aboard *Yankee* and leaves the same.'

Walking through an open grassy playground towards Shoreham Riverbank on England's south coast, you catch sight of a military cockpit and mast emerging through a gap in the hedge. Out of context like this, the 47.5m (156ft), cold, grey, angular German minesweeper is both austere and awe-inspiring, but the boat is the unlikely home of former mechanic Fred Cole and his family. This is their second houseboat in 35 years. When they purchased their first one, which sank in 2003, they didn't intend to live permanently on the water, but it was cheaper than buying a house. They moved into a neighbour's boat until they found an alternative, dismantling the old boat to make room on their mooring for a new one.

The *Fische*, which toured the Baltic during the Cold War era, was one of a 30-boat fleet built for NATO in 1960. After viewing the ship, Fred had only two hours to make up his mind whether to buy or not. It was full of rainwater and piles of rubbish, but it was spacious and the decision was made. He phoned his wife Polly to tell her he'd bought it.

Once the boat had been surveyed and insured, it began its expensive journey along the coast on tow from Southampton to Shoreham. However, its sheer size caused difficulties for the local council, which insisted that Fred needed planning permission to replace one boat with another, even on the same mooring. After an 'unpleasant and expensive fight', which lasted two years, Fred finally won this landmark case – no permission was required.

There are eight bedrooms as well as a separate flat for his son and granddaughter. Down in the hull is a large open space for the family to gather as well as for hosting local arts events related to the Shoreham Wordfest.

the minesweeper

style notes

This family home was created as a result of forward thinking. Fred and family are pioneers of the art of living on large vessels, and, in an extraordinary way, they have forged a unique approach to life on the water. In order to adapt a former naval vessel into a home, they had to make some amendments to the original space. The bridge is now their sitting room, and Fred cut out more porthole-style windows to increase the amount of light in the room. The original acrylic glaze was leaky and slightly opaque, so the windows were re-glazed with glass, which was more waterproof.

The renovation and transformation from a German warship to a home has been an enduring task. Clearing out the original contents – old manuals, obsolete equipment and piles of rubbish – took over four months, but it enabled Fred to fully appreciate the beauty of the ship's handsome naval architecture. The interior walls are now mainly whitewashed, with areas of exposed wood and tongue-and-groove panelling. The structural elements, such as the original sturdy staircases and huge metal doors, are peppered with the colours of family life, and a sense of belonging meets your every glance. Books are stored under the hull beams, while photographs and memorabilia line the dresser among the teapots, plates, pots and pans.

The style of this boat hinges on the evidence of everyday objects and the eclectic rumble of family life and fun. Authentically original with practical renovations and hand-rendered oddities, the minesweeper oozes a sense of creativity and intrigue. The hanging chains are almost ornamental yet their functionality is of utmost importance – they are used with a block and tackle to pull the boat onto the mooring. The wonderful juxtaposition of a family home inside the shell of a warship is such a bizarre and fantastic contradiction. As a visitor, you experience a sense of moving through a labyrinth of light and darkness, doors and corridors, steps and hatchways, ladders and walkways...

Down below, next to the stage, is Fred's workshop, an essential hub with a workbench stacked with bits of engine, nuts and bolts, screws, oily cloths and neatly stored hammers, which magnify the sense of sheer hard work and loving maintenance that a boat of this age and size requires. Upstairs, the deck functions as a roof terrace; pot plants and leather chairs are lined up alongside a collection of vintage bottles. With an overwhelming sense of authenticity and sincerity, the family's approach to life is refreshingly different – their style is about enjoying life, embellished with a sense of freedom and escape from the 'real world'. This is a true inspiration.

Few things in life have the unexpected visual surprise and intrigue to stop you dead in your tracks, but this extraordinary sculptural boat has the power to do just that. Modestly describing himself as a 'boat builder and renovator', Hamish McKenzie has created an inspirational and innovative home, although constant effort, labour and ingenuity are needed to keep this boat afloat...literally.

artist's home

The combination of unusual materials defies logic, context or original purpose. They are used for their form, material composition and creative expression. The *Verda* was originally a ferry, but it has morphed into an unexpectedly visually rich, dense and intriguing dwelling complete with an old coach, a three-wheeler Reliant Robin car, a washing machine, a fire engine, and even torpedoes. The list of identifiable re-used objects is seemingly endless. The practicalities, the engineering and the logistics of amalgamating these objects is awe-inspiring and beautifully eccentric.

Hamish began working on his first boat in 1986 and has worked 40-hour weeks ever since on his expanding fleet, moored on a tidal estuary on the south coast of England. He walks for miles and is inspired by what he finds: 'I always keep my eye out for stuff...I'm fascinated by forms and like to know how things fit together'. Animal skeletons and dried-out dead amphibians can be found on the walls and shelves of the interior as well as the exterior surfaces of the boat. For instance, he found a caravan made of fibreglass in the neighbouring woods and he knew that 'it would be good to use'. The accumulated effect of all these items echoes Gaudi's La Sagrada Familia, albeit on a smaller scale – an organic, evolving abundance of forms and colour.

style notes

The interior is a unique visual treat. Hamish has taken industrial, organic and everyday discarded items and interwoven them throughout. This is not about fashion or fad but is a unique form of personal expression, motivated by his fascination with how things work and compelled by his artistic endeavour. The collage of materials is extravagant and inspirational and rich with reds and oranges, animal prints, natural wood and flashes of green plants – all in warm hues and comfortable, homely tones.

The coach, including its wheels, was totally gutted before being transposed onto the boat, fitted with a parquet floor, tables and chairs, a human skeleton and a dartboard. Although seemingly abstract, these collected items tell their own story, and exactly where they were found has relevance to this boat. *Verda* boasts the remnants of at least seven other boats and inasmuch as inanimate objects can have a life, they live on.

The yellow petal-shaped windows in the bow are part of the boat's original architecture and have an art deco feel. An enormous industrial wood burner with a rocket-shaped flue heats the interior, and contrasting cushions in red, orange and animal print textiles are scattered on the circular window seat. The overall ambience is inviting, light and tranquil, but look closer and you will spot the animal skeletons, dried reptiles and amphibians that have been carefully placed to decorate the shelves and ceiling. Lush green plants flourish in the light that transcends the petal windows, reminding us of Hamish's love of organic form and the natural source of his inspiration.

soulful

Of all the boats featured in this book, these are the ones that bring the strongest interior design element to the mix. Not that *my cool...* is ever about the overtly unaffordable or unattainable. We occasionally take a peek at these, but we love the individual, the authentic, the expressive and creative homes.

The *Jolie* in Amsterdam's North Sea Channel is a home that, with half a chance, most of us would happily move into tomorrow. The owners have created something truly stunning yet homely in a massive boat. Undaunted by its size, they reduced its length by removing the middle section, and within that designed a flexible open-plan space where light and family life flow.

La Gondola, another converted freight barge in Amsterdam, is plywood-lined and a warm, welcoming space, complete with an inner open deck terrace area with outdoor bath and pear tree. And the London photographer's barge plies the Thames with grace, masculine warmth and charm. It doesn't shout, 'Look at me' but invites you into a comfortable beautiful world of worn leather sofas, a wood-burning stove and even a stylish dog.

And, of course, there's Tracey Metro and her *Retro Metro*, a 1970s-inspired weekend boat moored in Southern California and up-cycled thrift shop furnished. Bright and crisp, imbued with humour and great vintage style, both she and the boat have an incredible energy. It is a film-worthy beauty, lifting the spirits and showing what is possible with style, drive and vision underpinned with a good dose of thrift shop trawling. Happy times!

amsterdam houseboat

The *Jolie* is the second houseboat home for Bas, his partner Wendy and their two young children. This time round they wanted to create something amazing – their dream home. They already had the mooring on the outskirts of Amsterdam, which they had retained from the sale of boat number one. Bas, who has a company project-managing houseboat builds and conversions for people who want to live on the water, and his designer wife were both well qualified to create something special, having both vision and experience.

When they purchased the *Jolie*, a 50m (164ft) long freight barge there was a potential problem because the mooring was only 35m (115ft) long and, given that most of the locks they would travel through were of a limited size, they set about reducing the length of the boat. The central section was removed to reduce the length by 16m (52ft) and the two remaining pieces were welded back together. This may sound slightly alarming to the uninitiated, but for the Dutch, a nation of boat builders, lengthening and shortening boats isn't such an unfamiliar idea. The hull was in good condition, and although the boat was built in the 1930s as a barge to be towed without an engine it had been modified 20 or so years later and the engine fitted was still in good working order.

Luckily, the boat appealed to Bas and he was able to give it a new lease of life. He loved 'the lines, the hull – it was a classic, and the dimensions were good as was the engine. Being an interior and coastal waterways barge, it was relatively straight-sided and good for conversion – seagoing vessels usually have more curves and as it was used as a freight vessel it had a good volume, too. It was like starting with a clean sheet'.

style notes

It was really important for Bas and Wendy to retain the boat's original character on the exterior while creating an interior living space that would connect with the outside world. In particular, they wanted a terrace area, and rather than the boat being a top-lit space they decided to add windows along the sides of the vessel so they could see the horizon.

They wanted to create the feel of a loft-style apartment, which would be a comfortable space for their family. Bas had the project management skills while Wendy understands the nature of spaces. They both favoured a relatively open-plan format but the rooms had to feel good and not be cavernous or unfriendly, with suitable areas for them and their children to be doing different things simultaneously. Rather than running them off a long narrow corridor, they wanted them to link together in a flexible way. Their vision was for light to flow through the space and to create perspective and views. In its previous incarnation the boat had been a freight barge, so the hull was a cavernous dark space, with no windows. Stainless steel framed portholes and oblong windows were cut into the body of the ship and fitted with the most thermally efficient glazing available.

A main living area with kitchen and dining space was created on an upper level, leading via large folding doors onto the open terrace. Anxious to get as much light as possible into the below-deck areas of the ship, Bas and Wendy created a long narrow window at the end of the terrace. As well as being an attractive feature, it enables Wendy to keep a watchful

eye on what her children are up to if they're in a different room. 'If I'm sitting on the sofa, I can see what's going on in the kitchen, and as a safety measure I can watch the kids playing on the terrace – it's one of the best things we did, simple and effective.'

Their second premise was to create 'special' areas, each with their own character. The working wheelhouse is up high and fully glazed. Apart from its technical function when the ship is moving, it's a great place to sit and watch the outside world. The bedrooms at either end of the boat are simple yet functional. Appreciating the gorgeous soft Dutch light, and the difference between the tones in the mornings and evenings, they kept the walls principally white, adding spot colour as a means of defining a space. They felt that using more wholesale areas of different colour would create more visual separation.

Sustainability was an important consideration, and the boat is well insulated with glazed solar panels fitted to the roof of the wheelhouse. LED lighting was installed throughout and under-floor heating fitted beneath the oak floorboards. Two efficient wood burners were added, one in the sitting room and a smaller one in the kitchen/dining living space.

The *Jolie*, although it was initially designed for a very different purpose, feels right. Spacious, with good head height, long vistas and plenty of daylight throughout, it is a comfortable, beautiful and family-friendly space, and a testament to a very clever and technically proficient couple who have created a handsome and modern home.

They say a dog is man's best friend, but for one Londoner his pet proved to be a pretty good estate agent, too. Jim was walking his faithful pooch along the banks of the River Thames when the friendly animal spotted a potential playmate ahead. While the dogs gambolled along the riverbank, their two owners fell into easy conversation. The other man introduced himself as music mogul and former Elvis Costello manager Jake Riviera. Record life sounded exciting, certainly, but it was Jake's account of river life on his century-old Dutch barge that really hooked Jim. When Jake hinted that the vessel might be for sale, Jim didn't need much persuading.

The rest, as they say, is history – and history is what this boat has by the bucket load. This 29m (95ft) long and 5.5m (18ft wide) Hagenaar barge was built in 1905 in Groningen, Holland, deriving its name from its useful ability to squeeze under bridges in The Hague. Hagenaars also boast an up-going stern with accommodation underneath – a space-creating piece of engineering that makes them a popular choice as houseboats.

Jim's, however, has a few modifications that make his home thoroughly unique. Its gearbox was sourced from a World War II aircraft, while the engine came from a tank. Huge and heavy already, these additions could easily make it a virtual battleship, but Jim had other designs. A photographer by trade, he saw a quirky studio space instead. It sits in the heart of the boat – a beautiful glass workroom flooded by natural light. In contrast, the rest of the boat is a pretty picture of domesticity.

london photographer's barge

style notes

It's hard to get your head around the sheer volume of space. Jim's accommodation comprises three bedrooms and a roof deck garden – and that's just for starters. His studio is the beating heart of the boat: a white cabin-cum-light well, ceilinged by the sky and populated by gleaming white tables and chairs, which add to the luminosity and clarity of this special space. A jungle of plants creeps around the narrow metal spiral staircase, a nod to the boat's leafy mooring near the Royal Botanic Gardens at Kew. Up on deck, deep wooden planters surrounding an umbrella-shaded picnic bench underline the fact that this boat enjoys an enviable slice of London countryside. It's a tranquil spot that feels miles away from the hustle and bustle of the Big Smoke.

Back inside there is a sharp and extremely successful division of space from studio to living room. Rich brown tones and cosy panelling in the latter juxtapose the brightness of the former. It's a modern and bold interpretation of how to carve a new space in the heart of a turn-of-the century boat. The vessel's generous dimensions accommodate the dark scheme comfortably – a cluster of leather chairs creates a warm ripple of texture, which works well with the metallic surfaces of the filing cabinets.

Jim added the traditional Nestor Martin wood burner in this room. Such a large space calls for a focal point and this Belgian-built stove, with its decorative cast iron metalwork on a simple black-tiled tray, serves the purpose perfectly. Its pretty design also adds a touch of delicacy to an otherwise masculine interior.

The galley is that rare thing on a boat – it's wide and bright, encompassing a huge double-fronted oven, while storage needs are met by spacious cupboards. Echoing the living room, the warm, wooden surfaces imbue the kitchen with a homely charm and a sense of durability. This boat is built to last, but it has made concessions to domesticity, from the crowded herb racks to the hanging pots.

The wheelhouse is another beautiful element of this houseboat. Sympathetically decorated, the lemon bench cushions recall the flash of yellow from the angle-poise floor lamp in Jim's studio. Here, again, we can understand why a photographer would be drawn to this space. The large windows frame the panoramic views, offering us a snapshot of city living that we rarely see. No wonder even an experienced cameraman like Jim can put down his lens for a moment to admire the scene. City living doesn't get much better than this.

cabin on the water

If you're 2m (6ft 7in) tall, houseboat living isn't going to be the most comfortable arrangement in the world, but this didn't deter Dutch IT consultant Jack Beets when he and his wife Birgitte were looking to buy an old barge on the River Amstel. They figured that, at half the price of a terra firm home, they could afford to adapt it to their needs and vital statistics. And the fact that there was also room to throw in a sauna, cinema and motorboat mooring made the move even more inviting.

The couple drew up their own designs for the space. Cool and contemporary, their plans marked a departure from traditional Amsterdam houseboats. But a friend introduced them to the architect Ronald Hooft, who was more used to designing hip restaurants, and his ideas for a split-level interior and floor-to-ceiling glazing made the build still more ambitious. Jack fell in love with them and quickly signed up Ronald to create a modern masterpiece within the confines of the 60 sq m (645 sq ft) facade dictated by strict building regulations.

Of course, all this couldn't happen overnight and the build took two years to complete, with Jack and Birgitte effectively living on a floating construction site. The first two months were particularly trying, with the couple forced to curl up in the bedroom's walk-in wardrobe whenever they needed sleep. Slowly, however, their new home took shape and they could begin to appreciate the novel views and tailored design their houseboat haven affords. As they started to stretch out and unpack, the couple found other delightful benefits of being out-of-bounds on the water, such as turning the music up without worrying about neighbours.

style notes

Outdoor space is at a premium in any city centre residence, let alone one that's belted by water, so it's great to see how the Beets have factored in a roof terrace and a lower deck balcony, tied together by a bespoke geometric-patterned steel balustrade. Over time the red cedar cladding of the exterior walls will silver with age to nearly match the metal.

Inside, this high-spec houseboat is all about modern luxury and sculptural furnishings. In the living room a suspended fireplace faces a modular chocolate sofa, which nestles into the right angle of two walls. Meanwhile, a metal Plopp stool affords a stylish sit-down to take in the views across the water from enormous sliding doors out onto the balcony. The boat also makes some concessions to homeliness. The textured rugs, particularly the cowhide in the living room, bring character to the scheme. It's the same in the bedroom where a full-wall mural has been created from a holiday snap of the Guatemalan rainforest.

Open-plan living has become a popular way to maximise space and light on boats, but the danger is that interminable white surfaces and lack of clear delineation can make these areas bland and formless. Having different levels gave the Beets distinct zones to work with, and they've individualised these with colour and daring couplings of different materials. The bathroom effortlessly blends slate tiling on the floor and sides of the bath with a granite and walnut bespoke vanity unit. Here's a houseboat that's not afraid to be bold, and it has a lot of fun in the process.

la gondola

There is something about these old hard-working barges that demands our respect. Artist Laura and restaurant owner John were looking for a new houseboat, having outgrown their previous one, when *La Gondola* caught their eye – their family was expanding and they needed something bigger. It was a 40m (131ft) long Belgian Spitz Barge, which had just been pensioned off after a long life of hauling freight along the European river system.

The couple didn't demolish or refurbish the steering hut, deckhouse and machine room. They wanted the barge to remain navigable, so no alteration could be made to the engine, steering installation or anything relating to the safety and certification of the ship.

Laura and John engaged an architectural practice to create a light and airy home within this essentially industrial space. As with many of these types of conversions, the great challenge is to introduce light into the otherwise functional, large dark and cavernous space of the hull, which used to hold the cargo. The vessel needed to remain navigable, so 18 over-sized bronze watertight portholes were added and the space was transformed. At 5 x 30m (16 x 98ft), the cargo hold was huge, and at 3.2m (10ft 6in) high it was possible to fit a very spacious apartment or even a suburban house into this space. The hull was insulated with 10cm (4in) thick foam insulation and faced with light-coloured plywood. The floor was made of cast concrete on top of the insulation and pipework.

The main entrance is via a small patio just in front of the steering hut. The deckhouse and steering hut were restored and modernised without affecting their basic integrity and are now rented out as an independent mini apartment.

style notes

The striking features of this space are the harmonious effect of the warm-toned plywood finish throughout, and the incredible patio that has been created, which really is the stuff of dreams. It features a touch of private rural idyll in an outdoor bathtub combined with nature in the form of a fruit-bearing pear tree growing in a big tub. Luckily, the hefty base vessel is well accustomed to carrying huge tonnage and is more than capable of dealing with these weighty items. The safety of young children is always an issue of vital importance on any ship and a patio is an ideal way to provide them with an outdoor playroom without the risk of falling overboard.

The owners worked closely with the architects to create the interior, especially the kitchen. Laura's artwork graces the walls and John's restaurant expertise informed the design. The children sleep upfront in the prow where the mate had his small hut, and traditional woodwork and berth mean that this room exhales the atmosphere of the old ship. Further on along the corridor

are the bathroom and their parents' room, which is connected to the patio and illuminated by a skylight. This bears no resemblance to the bedrooms or cabins that you see on many ships and houseboats, where small bed bunks jostle for space – the room looks more like a light garden room.

The furnishings throughout the boat combine the eclectic, the beautiful and the interesting – an unusual mix of old and new pieces. The sharp red tiles in the kitchen and the yellow ones in the bathroom are a counterpoint to the light-coloured plywood lining the rest of the space. However, as a delicate and restful gesture the dining area is wallpapered, creating a simple yet clever visual and atmospheric change of style.

This boat is inspiring, expressive and powerful – a family home that embraces space, light, warmth and atmosphere, and the joy of the open-air bathtub on a summer's night would certainly have lifted the spirits of the toiling bargemen all those years ago in the boat's previous incarnation. It's an inspired conversion.

new york city houseboat

In the spirit of collectivity, Gabe Cohen and Jolie Signorile got together a group of six college friends, pooled their cash and together bought a rundown 1986-built houseboat. Their aim of creating a weekend retreat close to the city was noble, and I bet a great many of us have thought about and possibly talked about this but rarely followed through or achieved our dream.

The project required considerable planning and labour to get it off the ground at all. The boat had to be moved to a different location, but it had no engine and would have to be towed, and a lot of work was needed to renovate and refurbish it to modern standards. One member of the group, Morgan Evans, decided to look at the task as a whole to give all the other members a good grasp of the details and the magnitude of what they were taking on. He wisely drew a mind map with a charming but stylised hand-drawn houseboat at its centre – a conventional-style house literally sitting on a boat. Branches were drawn off it, each with the areas that needed consideration, including the funding of the project in its entirety, the running costs, the mission, its purpose as a whole, the legalities, and the contract between the parties concerned.

The boat was originally built in different social and economic times – an age of serious partying, of jacuzzis and wine fridges – as a party boat for a Goldman Sachs executive. But Gabe and Jolie are more modern souls, co-founders of the Brooklyn-based design company Fredricks & Mae; theirs is a clean modern aesthetic and, along with their friends, they approached the project with a strong work ethic but hoping to have some fun, too.

style notes

This space feels like a testimony to the spirit and energy of friends, furnishing it with items sourced on Craigslist as well as products from their own company, which specialises in design objects 'for the home, garden and sky'. The boat needed refurbishment, renovation and re-furnishing, and nearly all the old interior elements were ripped out. Cushions were re-upholstered, walls painted, the furniture neatly built in and storage added. Where original elements were good they were kept, such as the orange kitchen sink.

There are four bedrooms: three below deck and a larger one on the roof. Each sleeps two, but they are collegiate-shared spaces with no particular 'ownership'. Elements of the boat's environment were integrated into the overall design scheme with the wooden bar painted in a pattern inspired by what was the local boardwalk. Created and furnished with the intention of creating a relaxing environment, the boat also has a hammock to lie in.

The design is sensitive but inventive: the humble or overlooked is elevated and the everyday made beautiful. This space and the objects within it have a timeless quality and immediate warmth. And the project exudes sustainability and a willingness to work within a budget while pushing the boundaries creatively in terms of materials and collaboration.

This is a boat that has had past lives...it feels like a new incarnation, suited to the times and the modern lifestyle of its owners. She has been furnished lightly and delicately, and consequently is not stuffy, overcrowded or smothered in any way. This is an open, shared and restful space, which is sympathetic to the architecture of the vessel itself.

paris houseboat

It's a part of Paris the tourists don't often venture into – there are no *bâteaux mouches* here. Tucked just off the Seine, the Bassin de l'Arsenal feels strangely detached from the humdrum of the tree-lined boulevards above. It used to be a commercial port where goods were loaded and unloaded, but now it's a tranquil marina of 180 pleasure boats.

Stroll along the cobbled towpath and there is one vessel that might make you pause, painted a demure dark grey and capped towards the bow with an elegant white canopy, and you'll be struck by the unusual architecture of the upper deck: surely that's a train carriage grafted onto the back, a smokestack rising tall from its far end. Here's a place to dream of the city – and step out of it, too. Welcome to the home of Valérie Mazerat.

The in-demand designer/architect lives quietly here with her young daughter. Life afloat suits her so much that her office is also water-based and moored a short walk away. Valérie's domestic quarters are transporting in their simplicity and Seine-side romance. 'It's another world,' she agrees, 'which takes you far away from any semblance of the everyday. There is a sense of freedom you don't get living ashore, and time slows down.'

Maybe part of that comes from the way she has harnessed her effortlessly cool new Paris tastes to a heritage vessel (it was a working Dutch barge, built in the early 1900s). The train car addition from the 1920s has been kept albeit completely refurbished to house a living/dining space. The wheelhouse also lives on; a spinning globe dominates the control panel and you get the feeling that Valérie has allowed herself this little indulgence. It shouts of adventure, boldness and resolution, while her carefully curbed style elsewhere in the boat only whispers of such headiness.

style notes

The French expression *coup de foudre* has both a literal and figurative meaning. It describes a thunderbolt, but it is also commonly used to refer to that sudden head-over-heels shock of falling in love at first sight. Valérie's interior style is an intoxicating mix of both. Interspersing the earthy colour scheme are vivid injections of brightness, from the citrine galley curtains to the striped shopping bags hanging by the entrance. And it is full of romance, too – untamed in the natural fabrics she uses in her linens and soft furnishings, and more knowingly in the shy pinks that blush through the strict grey palette of the bedroom. A tactile sheepskin rug makes a soft cloud of the floor here, where elsewhere in the boat Valérie favours spartan stripped-down wooden floorboards.

Surprisingly for the home of a mother and daughter, there's a distinctly masculine feel to the barge. It is brought on, in part, as homage to the boat's industrial past. The galley fittings are a roll call of unfussy lighting and steel shelving, utilitarian pots and well-used chopping boards. The only concession is the elegant narrow shafts of the leg frames on the metal-topped catering table. Arne Jacobsen, one of the grandfathers of modern Danish furniture and functionalist style, is referenced in the simple vintage chairs surrounding it. Stacked stools are secreted at the end of a shelving unit and hint that, for all its austerity, this is a room which adapts well as a social space when friends and family are aboard.

A big illuminated Christmas star, taking up nearly an entire window, reinforces the potential for fun and festivity among friends.

Elsewhere in the boat there's something cinematic about the careful editing of personal effects against the sombre charcoal walls. Souvenirs from Morocco are particularly popular, from the living room Butterfly Chair sourced during a trip there, to the striking Berber portrait hanging above Valérie's desk, taken by photographer Serge Anton. In the bathroom the Moroccan influence is still more explicit, with travel mirrors and metal tumblers decorated with ornate hammered designs making for an exotic ship's head.

If sophisticated eclecticism is what you're after, let Valérie's Paris houseboat be your guide. She's created a serene canalside home spiced with rough industrial decor, mid-century period pieces and some splashes of North African influence thrown in for good measure. Combined, however, these elements make up an intoxicating design cocktail that is quintessentially Parisian. Her devil-may-care ensembles can be recreated by juxtaposing flea market finds alongside more modern pieces of furniture. Forget white walls – Valérie's colour palette is all repressed passion and exhilarating invention, controlled yet playful. Here's an example of houseboat design that moves beyond the shipshape – ship chic is what it's all about *en France*.

sausalito houseboat

Welcome to San Francisco – via Japan. *Wildflower* is a contemporary floating holiday home that's been baffling guests with its more traditional Asian past. It was designed in the 1970s by Japanese architect Kiddo, who hoped to bring a taste of his country's craftsmanship to the popular houseboat community of Sausalito by building a wooden structure entirely devoid of nails or noisy power tools, as used to be the custom in times gone by. His team of skilled workers measured, marked, hand-sawed, chiselled, chamfered, planed and joined the boat together to serve as his home from home.

Wildflower's current owners are Patricia and Daniel, who poetically describe its constantly changing views as 'waking up to a living postcard every morning'. Covering some 278 sq m (3,000 sq ft) and three storeys, it offers spacious living accommodation in a deep-water slip in Richardson Bay. In fact, so roomy is the houseboat that Patricia and Daniel now run it as a holiday let. To that end, they've completely redecorated the vessel, understanding that its natural light and relatively large proportions can easily accommodate richer tones and bold textile choices as well as a few quirkier additions, like the full-size tailor's model or the wall-hung sky-blue car door.

The couple both feel that change is a good thing. They've been through plenty of it aboard *Wildflower* already, learning not only how to sensitively redesign another man's dream but also how to live so close to the elements. Their biggest challenge wasn't picking out a colour palette or perusing soft furnishings but finding out how unstable their watery new foundations were by 'learning the lunar tides'.

style notes

The minimalist grace of traditional Japanese wood architecture is on display everywhere in this unique houseboat, but Patricia and Daniel single out the master bedroom as their favourite example. Here custom tatami mats and traditional sliding paper walls make it easy to believe that the mooring lines loosened during the night and the tide navigated *Wildflower* home to the Land of the Rising Sun. To give you a reality check, the bedroom's en suite includes a rain shower that opens onto an outdoor balcony with enviable Bay views.

While the couple were always keen to preserve the historic nature of the boat, they also knew that they wanted to give it a contemporary context. Their sons, both furniture designers, had a lot of input in the updated scheme, including wide Western-style white-upholstered armchairs and dining chair cushions with country-style ties. The most striking pieces, however, are tellingly movable.

Both the dining and over-sized coffee tables feature weathered timber boards on industrial castored steel frames. That the living and dining spaces can be so easily reconfigured is a nod not just to the nomadic possibilities of houseboat living but also to the way in which interior design has shifted over time to accommodate so many different elements.

Patricia and Daniel describe their scheme as 'rustic with a contemporary twist', which they've worked hard to blend into the heavily Japanese-influenced interior they inherited. Juggling the two is a potential minefield but, with a deft touch and spadefuls of creativity, they've managed to bridge not only decades but whole continents, too. Today, *Wildflower* enjoys the unique position of being an Eastern oasis in an artistic Californian enclave. There aren't many homes, even among the floating ones, that can be so adaptable.

california retro metro

Dreaming of the possibility of owning a second home and, like many of us, handicapped by budget constraints, the super-stylish American television DIY-er, designer Tracy Metro came across her inspiration and motivation in 'an old dry-docked 1960s houseboat that had similar lines to that of a Neutra house'. Following this glimmer of an idea, she started hunting for something similar, initially on the Internet but later on the road. Naturally thrifty and committed to 'up-cycling', Tracy soon recognised the benefit of going 'off grid' in the old-fashioned way and getting out there physically to find what she was seeking. On a trip to Northern California in the Sacramento Delta area, which is populated with many houseboats, she came upon a 1975 Harbor Master, now aptly christened *Retro Metro*.

The layout was just what she and her partner Marty wanted: a kitchen galley, a living room and a bedroom. 'The minute we crawled into the bedroom and saw the amazing orange curved and button-worked retro headboard, I knew we had found our boat.' The survey she commissioned revealed why the boat hadn't previously sold – it needed a new engine – but Tracy didn't want a boat that moved and the deal was done.

Now fully renovated and moored at its new home in Long Beach, California, Tracy describes the benefits of ownership as 'perfection' in terms of what the boat has given the couple. A 45-minute drive from their home, it's 'a getaway from the hustle and bustle of Hollywood. We both love the water, so from the minute we wake up to the minute we fall asleep, we're always looking at it, floating on it and swimming in it. As soon as we step aboard, our stress levels drop and we remember why we work...to enjoy life...and that's what we do aboard the *Retro Metro*. It's our haven, our bliss.'

style notes

When Tracy acquired it, the boat was filled with 'odd-ball furniture, such as a lazy-boy recliner chair, a futon, and other über-hideous pieces of furniture'. However, in spite of this, the amazing headboard in the bedroom and a few other stellar pieces, such as the bathroom light fitting and a Lucite doorknob, were winners. Tracy and Marty lived on the boat in all its hideousness for nine months while they figured out what to do; they felt daunted by the task ahead of them. Stripping the boat back to its bare essentials, they could sort out the utilities and install a proper shower where a sink cabinet had once been.

The 1970s was the inspiration for the boat and orange was the colour of the decade. It's Tracy's favourite, too, so it made perfect sense for her to use it throughout. Overall her design hook was a sleek retro finish. The walls, all clad with dark wood-panelled finishes, had to go and were replaced with the sheen and texture of white fibreglass panels. This makes the space feel open and crisp, even on the gloomiest of days. Tracy believes that light is a very important element in any design and 'the white reflects the light throughout the space, making it feel very inviting from the outside, even if I do say so myself!'

The bedroom cabin below deck is accessed by a small stairway. Tracy created a fold-down door, which closes over when not in use, with fitted upholstered cushions as an integral part of the living space. Cork flooring was fitted, and although it's faded by the sun, the look still works well with its retro appeal, and it's soft and comfortable underfoot.

The first big on-board project was the galley. By removing the two overhead cabinets, Tracy immediately lightened the space. She was determined to make full use of every available inch of space, and instead of the cabinet kickboards she fitted 15cm (6in) deep drawers beneath the cabinets to house all her 'bits and bobs' and avoid visual clutter. The countertops are a statement orange and were a costly part of the renovation. Tracy understands spaces, and to counteract the effect of the low ceiling height, she added a laminate thick edge to the worktops to make the counter feel visually weighty – needless to say, this and that glorious headboard are now her two favourite features.

Her hobby is 'thrifting' and this played an integral part in furnishing the boat – not just the furniture elements but also the small decorative items are secondhand. The only new purchase is the coffee table; having searched high and low for a table she liked, she eventually conceded and bought a new one. Tracy's approach is ethical design at its very best – bland mass production has been eliminated in favour of one-off finds. She has a passion for seeking out unusual objects that have been previously rejected, overlooked or confined to another decade.

This space is warm, playful and vibrant, but it's also sensitive. It has a delicacy and elegance – the retro pieces have carved out their own niche in a fresh new and modern way, landing in the twenty-first century with style and vigour. It is an outward expression of who Tracy is – happy, bold, creative, fun and thrifty. That's why it works!

sourcebook

architects and boat designers

+31architects
Amsterdam Watervilla
www.plus31architects.com

aarti ollila ristola architecture
Camley Street Viewpoint
www.aor.fi

duggan morris architects ltd
Floating Cinema
www.dugganmorrisarchitects.com

HOYT architects
La Gondola
www.hoyt.nl

k2s architects ltd
Finnish Floating Office
www.k2s.fi

moed & van gulpen
Welding and carpentry
www.moedvangulpen.nl

NLE
Makoko Waterfront Community
www.nleworks.com

PAD studio
Exbury Egg
www.padstudio.co.uk

pieter kromwijk and vivienne bancken
Netherlands Autarkhome
www.autarkhome.com

prast & hooft
Cabin on the Water
www.prasthooft.nl

robert nebolon architects
San Francisco Floating House
www.rnarchitect.com

sealander
Sea and land caravan
www.sealander.de

studio mjölk architekti
Prague Houseboat
www.mjolk.cz

waterloft.nl
Houseboat designers of the *Jolie*
www.waterloft.nl

interior designers

clio the muse
Upcycled vintage and designer furniture
www.cliothemuse.co.uk

tracy metro
LA Retro Metro
www.tracymetro.com

wendy rommers
The Jolie
www.wendyrommers.nl

artists and designers

brad hwang
Berlin Sculptor's Barge
www.bradhwang.com

jolie mae signorile and gabriel fredericks cohen
New York City Houseboat
www.fredericksandmae.com

sophie jamieson
Sophie & Kendall's London Houseboat
http://sophieillustrates.com

places to visit

berlin modern boat
www.welcomebeyond.com

berlin yoga boat
www.airbnb.com/rooms/1162525

the book barge
www.thebookbarge.com

camley street natural park
www.viewpointlondon.fi

copenhagen recycled
https://www.airbnb.co.uk/
rooms/2003116

ellis island ferry
www.yankeeferrynyc.com

the floating cinema
www.floatingcinema.info

the mirosa
http://www.thamesbarge.org.uk/
barges/barges/mirosa.html

pont 13 restaurant
www.pont13.nl

sausalito houseboat
https://www.airbnb.com/rooms/455025

word on the water
www.facebook.com/wordonthewater

charitable ventures

allotment on a barge
www.laburnumboatclub.com
www.Chug.org.uk

camley street viewpoint
www.architecturefoundation.org.uk/
programme/2012/floating-viewpoint-for-
camley-street-natural-park

www.wildlondon.org.uk

www.viewpointlondon.fi/en/articles/631-
camley-street-natural-park

exbury egg
www.spudgroup.org.uk

suppliers

genbyg.dk
Online store for reclaimed
building materials
www.genbyg.dk/en/contact_info/

windy smithy
Suppliers of handmade
wood-burning stoves
www.windysmithy.co.uk

credits

We would like to thank all the boat owners for allowing us to photograph their 'cool' houseboats.

Allotment boats www.laburnumboatclub.com, Chug.org.uk

Australian Sailing Boat Sophie Thé www.sophiethestylist.com
Instagram: sophiethestylist

Berlin Sculptor's Barge: Brad Hwang www.bradhwang.com, Elli Wedepohl, Joy Hwang, Lucy Hwang, Dr. Ernst Weihreter

William Borrell *Disco Volante*

Fred and Polly Cole www.shorehamhouseboats.co.uk

Copenhagen Recycled Jesper Holmberg Hansen, Jette Noa Liv Bøge, Sol Bøge Holmberg

Peter and Sally Dodds, *Mirosa*, Iron Wharf Boat Yard, ME13 7BY

Ellis Island Ferry www.yankeeferrynyc.com

La Gondola Laura de Monchy www.laurademonchy.com
John Hannema, owner of the restaurant, Het rijk van de Keizer www.hetrijkvanderkeizer.nl

Sarah Henshaw www.thebookbarge.com

Sophie and Kendall Jamieson http://sophieillustrates.com

Tracy Metro, Los Angeles, CA, TracyMetro.com, DomesticCircus.com

Netherlands Autarkhome Pieter Kromwijk and Vivienne Bancken www.autarkhome.com

Denis Oudendijk www.refunc.nl

Pont 13 www.pont13.nl

Bas van Schelven, owner of the houseboat company: www.waterloft.nl, Wendy Rommers, owner of design company: www.wendyrommers.nl, and daughters Lise van Schelven and Mette van Schelven

Paddy Screech and Jon Priverr www.facebook.com/wordonthewater

Sealander www.sealander.de

Jolie Mae Signorile and Gabriel Fredericks Cohen www.fredericksandmae.com

Imke Wangerin www.kongruenz.net, www.kongruenz-interkulturell.net, www.imkewangerin.wordpress.com

Welcome Beyond www.welcomebeyond.com

Clio Wood, upcycler and interior designer, through her label, Clio the Muse www.cliothemuse.co.uk

Woonark Wendy Alblas www.wendyalblas.com

All photography by Richard Maxted unless otherwise stated.
www.maxted.com
www.greenhousereps.com

Front cover	Jerome R. Rondeau www.flickr.com/photos/jrrondeau/
Pages 2–3	Nigel Rigden www.nigrig.com
Pages 10–11	Matthew Millman www.matthewmillman.com
Pages 12–13	John Sturrock www.johnsturrock.com Max Creasy www.maxcreasy.com
Pages 14–17	Nigel Rigden www.nigrig.com
Pages 18–21	Iwan Baan www.iwan.com
Pages 22–25	Matthew Millman www.matthewmillman.com
Pages 44–47	Photography: Sean Fennessy http://seanfennessy.com.au/ Styling: Lucy Feagins for The Design Files http://thedesignfiles.net/
Pages 48–51	Martin Tuma, BoysPlayNice www.boysplaynice.com
Pages 52–53	Jack Hobhouse www.jackhobhouse.com
Pages 58–61	Luke Forsythe www.lukeforsythe.co.uk
Pages 62–63	Jack Hobhouse www.jackhobhouse.com
Pages 72–75	Barbara Zonzin www.barbarazonzin.com
Pages 76–77	Lars Franzen
Pages 88–91	Gianni Bassi www.vegamg.it
Pages 92–95	Photography: Anouk De Kleermaeker www.studio309.nl Styling: Yvonne Bakker
Pages 96–97	Mika Huisman www.decopic.com Marko Huttunen www.markohuttunen.com
Pages 104–105	Denis Oudendijk
Pages 106–109	Navid Baraty www.navidbaraty.com
Pages 120–121	Douglas Lyle Thompson www.douglaslylethompson.com
Pages 126–129	Eddy Pearce www.locationpartnership.com Jim Naughten www.jimnaughten.com
Pages 130–133	jansje@jkf.nl www.jkf.nl www.taverne-agency.com www.jkf.wetransfer.com
Pages 134–137	Luuk Kramer www.luukkramer.nl
Pages 138–141	Douglas Lyle Thompson www.douglaslylethompson.com
Pages 142–145	Richard Powers www.richardpowers.co.uk
Pages 146–149	BESSFRIDAY Photography	bessfriday.com	310.266.5641
Pages 150–155	Still photography provided courtesy of Scripps Networks, LLC Daniel Collopy www.danielcollopy.com

Additional captions: page 1 amsterdam houseboat; pages 2–3 exbury egg; page 4 sophie and kendall; page 6 word on the water; page 9 the book barge; pages 10–11 san francisco floating house; page 26 sophie and kendall; pages 52–53 floating cinema; page 78 berlin modern houseboat; pages 98–99 the minesweeper; pages 120–121 new york city houseboat; page 157 copenhagen recycled boat and the book barge; page 160 sophie and kendall.

acknowledgements

Writing and art directing these books is a privilege that opens up whole new worlds of the creative endeavours of others, both of the boat-owning contributors and the team behind the books.

Thank you to all the owners, for making us feel welcome and allowing us to photograph their properties and to dip into their worlds for a while. I am enlightened and very grateful.

To Fiona Holman at Pavilion Books, the strength behind the project, and the hardworking and conscientious team, Heather, Emily, Rachael and Sarah, thank you all very much.

I was lucky again to have the joy of working and shooting with Richard Maxted, seeing the lovely images emerge on the back of the camera, and having some fun along the journey, too. I feel very fortunate to have had such an experience.

These books now have a huge overseas market as well as a domestic one, and I appreciate all the readers who have been tempted to pick up and buy a copy. I hope that the optimism and spirit of the books resonate with you all.

And, finally, my family. I appreciate your tolerance at my being consumed with concentration and spending late nights and weekends getting this book into shape. I can happily share with you this finished product and the happiness it brings.

Jane Field-Lewis

Jane Field-Lewis is a stylist for film, photography and TV and is also the creative consultant behind the hit C4 series *Amazing Spaces*. Her work is truly global – both her styling work and books are internationally successful. She has written and art directed *my cool caravan*, *my cool campervan*, *my cool shed* and *my cool kitchen* and co-authored with the architect and television presenter George Clarke the books to accompany the *Amazing Spaces* TV series.

She has an enduring love for people and style, believing that the two are closely entwined. Her career is based on the aesthetic, whether high- or low-style, and across people and objects.

With her styling work, *Amazing Spaces* and *my cool...* she hopes to inspire an affordable, individual and creative approach to any project.

First published in the United Kingdom in 2015 by
Pavilion
1 Gower Street
London WC1E 6HD

my cool® is the registered trademark of Jane Field
(UK TM registration no. 2575447).

Copyright © 2015 Pavilion Books Company Ltd
Text copyright © 2015 Jane Field-Lewis

Editorial Director Fiona Holman
Photography by Richard Maxted
Styling by Jane Field-Lewis
Design Steve Russell
Editor Heather Thomas

ISBN 978-1-909-10886-8

A CIP catalogue record for this book is available from the British Library.

10 9 8 7 6 5 4 3 2 1

Reproduction by Tag Publishing (UK)
Printed and bound by 1010 Printing International Ltd in China

This book can be ordered direct from the publisher at
www.pavilionbooks.com